WIDE WORLD OF WEIRD

over 100 reports of high strangeness

By M. Belanger

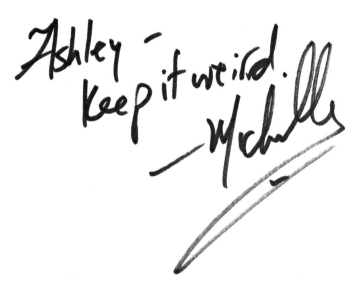

Inspiration Press ❖ Oberlin, OH

M. Belanger

The Wide World of Weird is © 2019 by Michelle Belanger

No part of this book may be reproduced in any form, physical or electronic, without prior permission from the author, with the exception of short passages for the purpose of review.

All rights reserved

First Printing. First edition

Author photo is © 2019 by Jax Edwards

Published by Inspiration Press
a division of the Temple of Wisdom
36 South Street, Oberlin, Ohio 44074

ISBN: 9781653925544

In Memoriam

This book is dedicated to the memories of Nick Reiter of the Avalon Foundation and Hans Holzer, the original ghost-hunter. It was a pleasure to meet and trade theories with you both during your sojourn on this earthly plane. Ave atque vale.

M. Belanger

TABLE OF CONTENTS

Introduction	9
Merlin's Arms	13
Dream Revelations	15
The Ringcroft Poltergeist	19
Haunting Melodies	22
Ubiquitous Crybaby Bridge	24
The Mysteries of Hangar 18	26
It's in the Cards	28
The Eternal Warrior	30
The Psychology of the Paranormal	32
The Indubitable Charles Fort	35
The Bentwaters UFOs	37
Ancient Echoes of War	39
The Mystery of the Watchers	41
Chicago's White Lady	44
Fire in the Sky	45
Rapping with the Spirits	48
Oak Island: Digging Deeper	54
Great Balls of Fire!	56
Where Little Green Men Come From	58
Fever Dreams	60
Nine Tenths of the Law	61
The Bell Witch	63
Call Him Corpsedancer	68
Nightmare in the Skies	69
American Vampires	71
All Hallows' Hags	73
The Work of the Devil	74
Come Have a Ball at Myrtle Hill	76
Telepathic Theory of Apparitions	78
What's Your Color?	85

The Way of the Secret Masters	87
Witness to Murder	89
The Magi of the Drawing Room	92
The Lady from Heaven	94
Kansas City Vampire Cult	97
The Blood Countess	100
The Ghost's Afoot!	104
Edison's Quest to Talk to the Dead	106
But How Much for the Postage?	108
Dancing with Death	110
The Haunting of Jackson Square	112
Does My Insurance Cover It?	113
Capturing the Light of Life	115
The Father of Ghost-Hunting	117
Retooling Paranormal Technology	119
Poe's Grim Prophecy	121
Is Hi Tech the Best Tech?	123
The Groovy Art of Stereomancy	125
The Mysterious Cat	127
Mapping the Unknown	129
The Weeping Woman of the Rio Grande	132
Falling Off the Edge of Time	135
What Has Two Eyes, No Mouth and a Melon Head?	137
Haunting the Internet Since 1999	141
Art from Beyond the Grave	143
Christopher Columbus Discovers a UFO	145
The Lantern Man	147
The Borley Rectory Haunting	149
Out of Thin Air	151
Maps of Atlantis	153
Come on Baby, Light My Fire	155
Terror in the Night	156
Harbinger of Doom	158

Dream a Little Dream	160
Hunting Ghosts Can Be a Drain	161
Mind the Tommyknockers	162
Hinckley's Library Ghost	165
Out of Body, Back in Five	166
Stranger Than Fiction	168
A Mother's Last Goodbye	170
Mysteries of the Great Pyramid	172
Faerie Changelings	174
Jung at Heart	176
Are We There, Yeti?	177
A Meeting by Midnight	179
Something Banging in Bingen	180
X-Files on the Emerald Isle	181
MUFON's Hollywood Hook-Up	182
The Dark Secrets of Solomon	183
The Great Ladybird Invasion of 1869	186
To Orb or Not to Orb	188
Ghost-Spotting	190
Phantoms and Feast Days	191
Ghosts Over Roswell	193
The Haserot Angel	194
Biblical Bloodsuckers	196
The Demons of Dr. Faust	197
Ouija Board: On the Books	199
Would the Real Vampire Please Stand Up?	202
The Grand-Daddy of Goth	204
Paranormal Obsession	206
Faeries, Ghosts, and Aliens	208
Ghosts and Graveyards	211
Top Five Haunted Cities	212
Dreams and Psychic Experience	214
The Mysterious Dr. Rudd	216
Here There Be Dragons	219

Omens of Death	221
Dreamwalking and Deathbed Visitations	223
A-Ghosting We Will Go!	224
Fetches, Wraiths, and Doubles	226
Sailing the Ship of Dreams	229
Harvard's Black Mass	231
Angels to Some…	234
Faerie Tricksters	236
Dead Mountain	238
About the Author	241

INTRODUCTION

When I was a kid, I practically lived at the library. Fortunately, my home town of Hinckley had a pretty awesome one (bonus: it was haunted). Almost as soon as I could read, I gravitated toward books about weird topics: witches, ghosts, UFOs, monsters. I was a weird kid, and lucky for me, my family was fine with it. Anything that was strange and a little mysterious held my attention.

Back then, in the late 70s and early 80s, there was a lot of interest in the weird and mysterious, and books on those topics proliferated. Some of my favorites were these big coffee-table volumes published by groups like Time-Life Books and the Reader's Digest. These thick hardbacks were filled to brimming with single-serving stories of ghostly encounters, psychic experiences, UFO sightings, and everything else in between. The way the articles were written, they gave you the most exciting details of every case, lingered on elements that raised eerie questions, and, in the end, generally left it up to the reader to decide how much they wanted to believe.

I ate those things up. Having access to those volumes ignited my imagination and helped to inspire my earliest inquiries into the paranormal. Periodically, I go back and re-read the ones I still own, and I always discover some new and fascinating angle I'd previously missed.

This volume is my personal homage to those old "Mysteries of the Unknown" books. The articles collected here span about a decade of my writing, mainly for publications like *Alternate Perceptions* (1996-1998), *Fate Magazine* (1998-2010), and the *Paranormal Insider* (2007-2009).

Of these publications, the vast majority of articles are drawn from the *Paranormal Insider*. This was a paranormal blog established specifically as an online resource published in tandem with episodes of *Paranormal State*. I was freelancing for the blog long before I was ever on the show, along with Rosemary Ellen Guiley and several other paranormal researchers.

One of the things I really loved about the *Paranormal Insider* was the variety of writing the blog encouraged. We had a range of topics each week and we were each assigned two to three of these topics at random. The subject matter changed with every cycle, as did our assignments. This kept the blog from getting stale, and it also challenged each of us to venture out of our comfort zones with every release. For me, that meant writing about UFOs and cryptids in addition to pieces on hauntings and psychic experiences. I always had a blast doing the research.

Because the *Paranormal Insider* blog was intended as entertainment, we were encouraged to write with a style that was journalistic but also a little light-hearted, with an emphasis on curiosity and mystery. It was exactly like those single-serving entries in the big books I'd loved as a kid. It was a really great experience.

After the first year, of course, I ended up on camera with *Paranormal State*. After that, as my involvement on the show increased, I had less time to devote to my paranormal journalism. The blog was eventually shut down, but I saved every article I had published in those years.

I have collected those articles as well as many others here with very little editing, primarily because I want to preserve the unique voice and flavor of the times. This means that a few details are not exactly up to date: my article on Hans Holzer, for example, written not long after meeting him at a PRS event, still speaks of him in the present-tense. The same goes for Nick Reiter of the Avalon Foundation, who was the first paranormal investigator to work with me back in the 90s. Both have since passed on.

There is also an amusing-in-retrospect article on the prophecies surrounding 2012 and, while I briefly considered excluding this, I think it's fun just to see how those thoughts held up over time.

Fortunately, most of the other topics covered in this book are matters of history (or at least, folklore), and so the stories told in each entry are reasonably timeless. The articles cover a vast geography of weird: mysterious sightings of yetis in the Himalayas; Lord Byron's alleged powers of bilocation; techniques of aura photography; backwoods poltergeists; prophetic dreams; even ancient Egyptian reports on UFOs. In fact, the only certain thread each article has in common is an element of high strangeness.

That high strangeness – and the lure of the mysterious it inspires – is what has always kept me coming back to this subject matter. Who can resist the suggestion that our reality is far more complicated than many of us might be comfortable admitting, that our minds are more powerful than we acknowledge, and that our world contains hidden pockets of wonder that we have yet to fully explore?

I know I can't. If you're reading this, you probably can't resist either. So, let us explore a world of wonder together, where endless possibilities exist just beyond the horizon and every shadow holds some secret waiting to be found.

M. Belanger
Dec. 31, 2019

MERLIN'S ARMS

In the Vale of Glamorgan in rugged Southern Wales you can find a stretch of coast with the second highest tidal range in the world. Along this coast is Barry's Island (Welsh: *Ynys y Barri*), and a myth surrounds a cleft in the nearby rocks. This legend goes back at least to the time of Episcopalian minister Robert Kirk who lived in the 1600s.

Kirk lived in Aberfoyle, in Scotland. Born in 1644, in modern times, he is best known for his 1691 publication, *The Secret Commonwealth,* although the book wasn't published until after his death. *The Secret Commonwealth* is a book about the reality of faeries, and it collects a vast array of legends and encounters with the Little People of the British Isles. In the case of his entry on *Ynys y Barri,* the faerie lore intersects with another quintessential legend of Great Britain: the tales of King Arthur and his wizard, Merlin.

As the story goes, if you should climb the rocks at *Ynys y Barri* and press your ear against the cleft you find there, you will hear the ceaseless industry of the folk beneath the hill. Just beyond the slim feature in the rocks, their forges roar, and their billows puff. They strike metal with their hammers, shaping arms and armor day and night and the endless clamor resounds beyond the rocks.

Centuries before, they were tasked to forge arms for Aurelius Ambrosius, a legendary war-leader who fought against the Anglo-Saxons in the 5th century. Merlin himself bound the entire faerie tribe, and that binding compels them to keep working until the great wizard himself gives the word to cease.

Of course, Merlin is long dead. There is no one left alive to release the faeries from their labor, and so they hammer endlessly in their hidden fortress beneath the hill.

Dream Revelations

Our dreaming minds can reveal a great deal. With invaluable pathways to unconscious knowledge and memories, dreams can be harnessed to access secrets we don't even realize that we know.

Thomas Edison actively used his dreaming mind to trouble-shoot inventions when he otherwise got stuck, and he was hardly alone in finding both inspiration and revelation in his dreams. Elias Howe, inventor of the lockstitch sewing machine, famously had his final design of the needle come to him in a dream. Similarly, Friedrich August Kekulé, the German chemist who determined the structure of benzene, had this information manifest first in his dreams.

Scientists and inventors are not the only ones to have benefited from revelations accessed by their unconscious minds during dreams. 19th century Assyriologist Dr. Hermann V. Hilprecht had a dream that helped him solve a puzzle surrounding a set of Babylonian artifacts – and either this solution came from the depths of his own unconscious mind or he was visited in his sleep by the guiding spirit of an ancient Mesopotamian priest. The professor himself was never quite sure.

The story begins in 1892 at the University of Pennsylvania. Dr. Hilprecht was a professor of Assyriology there. Previously, the university had sponsored an expedition to several locations significant to the history of Babylon, including Nippur, where a grand temple to the god Bel once had stood. Dr. Hilprecht was responsible for sharing the latest findings on the artifacts recovered by the expedition in his new book, *The*

Babylonian Expedition of the University of Pennsylvania, Series A: Old Babylonian Inscriptions Chiefly from Nippur. By mid-March, the proofs had arrived, and Dr. Hilprecht was expected to make any minor changes he deemed necessary, then approve the proofs for the publisher.

Except there were two artifacts that troubled him.

The artifacts in question were small rings of agate, of which only fragments remained. Dr. Hilprecht hesitantly identified the objects as finger-rings. Based on their partial inscriptions, the professor dated them to the Kassite period of Babylonian history, between 1700 and 1140 BCE. One of the fragments had a syllable on it that suggested a connection with King Kurigalzu, circa 1300 BCE, although this interpretation was tentative at best. Part of the professor's problem was that he was working from field drawings of the fragments and not the objects themselves. The actual pieces of agate were housed in a museum in Istanbul. With the deadline from his publisher fast approaching, Dr. Hilprecht had to make his decision about what his book would say about these fragments. Ultimately, he decided to mention Kurigalzu for the one but the other he consigned to the vast number of unclassified Kassite pieces.

He was exhausted from his day as well as the protracted search. Still not 100% satisfied with his interpretation on these two pieces, he nevertheless signed the proof sheets.

And then he went to sleep.

In his dreams, Dr. Hilprecht was visited by a strange figure from the past. The man was tall, about forty years old, and dressed in a simple tunic. From his features, clothes, and coloration, the professor identified him as a priest from the Babylonian era.

The ancient priest approached the professor and beckoned him to follow. When Hilprecht stepped after the priest, he found himself traveling backwards into the past until they stood together in a low-ceilinged room with no windows. Fragments of lapis lazuli and agate covered the floor and a large wooden chest stood to one side. Professor Hilprecht felt that he had arrived in the ancient Temple of Bel, long before the walls of the place had crumbled to dust.

As the professor marveled at his surroundings, the robed priest turned to him and explained the history of the two fragments that had so puzzled the professor during his waking hours. These were not finger rings, but pieces of what had once been a votive cylinder. According to the priest, the cylinder had been a gift to the Temple of Bel from King Kurigalzu, but it had been cut into three separate pieces when that same king issued an order for the priests to construct a pair of agate earrings for the statue of the god Ninib, son of Bel.

Only two of those pieces had been found by the University of Pennsylvania's expedition. The ancient priest insisted that the third ring would never be uncovered. Dr. Hilprecht was further told that he would confirm the truth of the story if he looked at the edges of the two fragments and put them back together. The inscription would become clearer once the two portions were reunited. After imparting this message, the priest disappeared.

Hilprecht woke with the dream fresh in his mind, immediately writing it down in every detail. Astounded and elated by his night-time expedition, he recounted the whole experience to his wife. The next day, he re-examined the fragments. Sure enough, they could be pieced together and, in doing so, their inscription became clear: *"To the God Ninib, son of Bel, his Lord, has Kurigalzu, Pontifex of Bel, presented this."*

When he told his friend Professor William Romaine Newbold, however, Newbold pointed out a possible problem. In the original descriptions of the fragments recorded by the archaeologist Dr. John Peters, the two agate fragments were different colors. Newbold worried that this meant they couldn't possibly have been part of the same object. Hilprecht wasn't so sure.

Later that summer he had the opportunity to examine the fragments directly. He visited Istanbul and traveled to the museum where the objects were housed. There he met with Halil Bey, the director of the museum. After recounting his dream to Bey, they both examined the fragments together. Just as Dr. Peters had initially observed, the pieces were different colors of agate. However, it was banded agate, and closer inspection revealed that the cylinder had been cut almost perfectly along one of the lines of color.

The two pieces were unmistakably part of the same object. Dr. Hilprecht's dream was confirmed – although whether the Priest of Bel had been a convenient manifestation of his unconscious mind or a three-thousand-year-old ghost, even Hilprecht couldn't say.

The Ringcroft Poltergeist

Poltergeists are so-called "noisy spirits" that are believed to have the power to transport objects through the air, throwing small items, knocking breakables off of shelves and, in the modern age, interfering with electronic devices – typically in destructive ways.

In the past, poltergeist phenomenon was generally attributed to the activity of a spirit. Sometimes, this spirit was thought to be non-human – either demonic or, in some instances, fey. In more recent times, the general opinion of poltergeist phenomenon has changed toward a theory involving the central living person involved in the poltergeist case itself. Such an individual is called a "nexus" (at least in the writings of paranormal investigator Harry Price) and is seen to be the actual cause of the movement of objects through a latent and largely unconscious form of telekinesis. It is widely held in current paranormal thought that the living human nexus of poltergeist phenomenon is typically a young girl around the age of puberty, and something inherent in the tumultuous hormonal and emotional shifts associated with puberty is responsible for setting off or fueling the phenomenon.

Although most modern readers probably learned of poltergeist phenomenon through a series of movies from the 1980s -- most notably the eponymous *Poltergeist* with haunted child Carol-Anne, poltergeist phenomenon has been recorded for hundreds (if not thousands) of years. One interesting tale of early poltergeist phenomenon is recorded in *Scotland, Social and Domestic: Memorials of Life and Manners in North Britain* a book written by Rev.

Charles Rogers and published in 1869. It tells of the famous Ringcroft Poltergeist. This was an ongoing phenomenon in the parish of Rerrick, Scotland in the late 1600s. The full quote on the case (from p. 246 of the Rogers text) appears below:

> "During the months of February, March, and April, 1695, the house of Andrew Mackie, mason, Ringcroft, parish of Rerrick, Kirkcudbrightshire, was the scene of strange procedure. Stones and missiles of all kinds were thrown into the house as by an invisible hand. Voices were heard uttering denunciations and warnings, and adjuring repentance. Missives written with blood were strewn about the premises. Members of the family were beaten with invisible rods, and dragged about mercilessly. The neighboring clergy assembled, and subscribed a declaration certifying the phenomena."

Rogers himself was quoting from earlier sources recorded by the minister overseeing the investigation. Rev. Alexander Telfair, minister of the parish of Rerrick in the Stewartry of Kirkcudbright, was called in by Mackie to put an end to the mysterious events harrowing his family. Telfair attempted to clear the infestation with prayer and fasting, but mostly got bludgeoned about the head by flying stones for his trouble. In the end, five other ministers in addition to Telfair got involved, as well as the blacksmith and several other laymen, but no amount of fasting, prayer, or other attempts could still the ghostly activities. Eventually the phenomenon ceased on its own, inspiring Telfair to conclude his narration of the events with these words:

> "Now all things aforesaid being of undoubted verity, therefore I conclude with that of the Apostle, I. Peter v., 8-9 – Be sober, be vigilant, because your adversary the devil, as a roaring lion, walketh about seeking whom he may devour. Whom resist steadfast in the faith."

The parting quote makes it abundantly clear what Telfair felt the family had been dealing with throughout that strange spring in 1695.

Haunting Melodies

The Devil is a fiddle player. At least, that's what we learn in the classic song, "The Devil Went Down to Georgia." Here, the Devil appears to challenge a young fiddle player named Johnny. Johnny, according to the song, is "the best that ever was," and he knows it – so the Devil takes advantage of his sinful pride, betting him a golden violin if Johnny can outplay Old Scratch. The song is a rousing mix of story and melody, and it draws upon a well-established tradition in southern folklore where the Devil shows up to wage a bet for a boastful person's soul.

The Devil's connection with the violin is much older than this 1979 Charlie Daniels Band song, however. Around 1749, the Devil reportedly appeared to a real-life fiddle player and offered a pact. The "fiddle" player was none other than renown Baroque violinist, Guiseppe Tartini. Tartini was a composer in addition to being a master of the violin, and he created one of his most breath-taking works after a very peculiar dream.

While Tartini slept, he dreamed that the Devil appeared to him and made a pact. As part of the pact, the Devil did whatever Tartini would bid him. Curious about the Devil's skill on his favorite instrument, Tartini handed Old Scratch his violin and asked him to play. In the dream, the Devil reported admitted that he could manage a few tunes, and then proceeded to play a sonata that left Tartini utterly dumbfounded. In Tartini's own words recording the event: "...imagine my surprise when I heard a sonata so unusual and so beautiful, performed with such mastery and intelligence, on a level I had never before conceived was possible!"

Tartini was so overcome with the beauty and mastery of the Devil's violin work in his dream that he awoke gasping for breath. He immediately took up his violin in the waking world and struggled to recreate the infernal melody of his dream. Although Tartini felt that he did not even come close, the resulting sonata is considered a masterwork. Tartini called it *The Devil's Trill*, and anyone who's attempted to play it will admit that it seems almost inhuman in its complexity.

Ubiquitous Crybaby Bridge

Crybaby Bridge is a haunted location often frequented by area teens looking for a spooky thrill later at night. As the story goes, a local girl had an unwanted baby, and, in despair, she walked to the bridge and threw the infant to its death. At night, you can still hear the unfortunate baby wailing miserably, its spirit unable to find rest because of its terrible demise. The haunted bridge is located in Columbus, Georgia.

But wait! It's also in New Hope, Pennsylvania. And there are no less than twenty-four haunted locations known as Crybaby Bridge in the state of Ohio alone. What gives?

In some of the stories connected with the haunted bridge, the mother did not throw the infant to its death below, but instead was walking along with her child and fell to her own death with the baby still in her arms. A few of the hauntings get more elaborate than merely involving claims of ghostly wailing. Some suggest that if baby powder is sprinkled along the bridge, the footprints of a small child will show up. Other visitors of so-called Crybaby Bridges claim to have discovered the prints of tiny hands on the hoods or sides of their cars once they have driven away.

Given the profusion of Crybaby Bridge locations, it's obvious that this haunting is more of an urban legend than a ghostly fact, and yet again and again, people who visit these locations report real phenomenon. Investigators at the Columbus, Georgia version of Crybaby Bridge even brought back some fairly clear EVP. So, what exactly is going on with all these crybabies?

One possibility has less to do with distraught mothers who drown their infants and more to do with the nature of bridges themselves. Much like a crossroads, a bridge is an in-between place. It is something that leads from one place to the next. As a mythic symbol, a bridge is then neither here nor there – a perfect location for spirits that do not properly belong to our earthly realm to cross over, if only for a little while. Notably, in Voodoo, there is a minor Loa, known as Ti Jean Quinto, who reputedly lives under bridges.

Haunted bridges are not just an American phenomenon, and many of the stories can be traced back to ancient times. All the tales of haunted bridges contain the same mythic, universal elements as all of the Crybaby Bridge stories. Perhaps, in the end, we just have a gut response to bridges that deals less with spirits and more with psychology, but perhaps there's something to be said about that "between the worlds" idea after all.

THE MYSTERIES OF HANGAR 18

Dayton, Ohio is not a remarkable town. Few folks outside of Ohio might have even heard of it, if not for the presence of the Wright-Patterson Air Force Base. This military base started life merely as Wright Field (so named for the Ohio-born brothers who invented modern aviation). Allegedly, not long after the UFO crash at Roswell, NM, all of that changed. Material from the New Mexico crash is believed to have been transported to Dayton, whereupon Wright Field became Wright-Patterson Air Force Base.

Many UFOlogists believe that, since that fateful summer in 1947, Wright-Patterson has been used to store not only wreckage from downed alien craft but also bodies of the aliens themselves. It was not long before rumors began to circulate about the mysterious "Blue Room," or, more widely, about Hangar 18. Stories about this top-secret location in the Air Force Base were so persistent that in the 1960s, Senator Barry Goldwater of Arizona dropped in on the base and sought permission to view Hangar 18 from General Curtis LeMay. His request met with quite a stir at the base itself and was flatly denied by LeMay.

A variety of credible witnesses have come forth claiming to have seen some of the bizarre things stored at Wright-Patterson. Norma Gardner, who had worked at the base for a number of years and held a high security clearance, claimed to have been responsible for photographing, tagging, and cataloging materials recovered from crashed saucers. She also claimed to have seen the bodies of two aliens on at least one occasion.

Physicist Robert Sarbacher, a consultant to the Department of Defense's Research and Development Board made a startling statement to a group of Canadian scientists on September 15, 1950. He affirmed that the US government had alien materials in its possession and further, that it had been trying to duplicate their performance, albeit without success.

Retired Air Force officer Arthur Exon has testified that alien crash remains were brought to Wright Field while he was serving there in 1947. Exon later became a brigadier general and, in 1964, he was named the Wright Patterson base commander. Even with this high rank, he was still denied direct access to any of the studies being carried out upon the alien material. Exon also asserted that among the materials gleaned from the 1947 crash were alien bodies, and these were also under study at Wright Patterson. He remains the highest-ranking military person to come forward with statements regarding the Roswell crash.

Given all of these accounts, it seems highly credible that something top secret was, at least at one time, going on at Wright Patterson. But does the Dayton base still harbor the mysterious materials in Hangar 18? One retired Air Force pilot, speaking under the condition of anonymity, told UFO researcher Leonard Springfield that at least some of the items originally stored at Wright Patterson were later moved to a site in Colorado Springs.

Even if nothing extra-terrestrial remains at the Ohio Air Force Base, the legend of Hangar 18 has become such an iconic part of modern UFO mythology that rumors about what's really there are likely to continue indefinitely.

It's in the Cards

Circle. Square. Star. Circle...

You've seen them flashed on episodes of the *X-Files* and on the covers of *Time Life Books*. They're a deck of simple shapes, black against white, five images total. Some people know them as Rhine cards, after Dr. JB Rhine, the founder of the Rhine Institute and a pioneer in modern parapsychology. However, Dr. Rhine himself originally named them after his assistant, Karl Zener.

Zener cards are designed to test psychic abilities. Telepathy, clairvoyance, and even precognition can be measured with this deck – or at least, statistical anomalies in an individual's mean accuracy can strongly suggest that something more than random chance is going on.

For years, Rhine and Zener experimented with these cards, amassing statistics to prove that humans have a kind of sixth sense. Although many scientists still refuse to recognize the significance of parapsychological research, Rhine and Zener nevertheless proved that something real was going on with their subjects who were able to accurately identify the images on these cards, sight unseen.

The cards are designed with simple, iconic images so there can be less likelihood of an image getting confused with something else during the process of transmission. The idea is for the individual who holds the deck and is looking at each card in succession to try "sending" these images to a receiver. The receiver may be in the next room or they may be miles away. Theoretically, with such powers as telepathy, proximity really doesn't matter. The key instead lies in the psychic connection between two minds.

Similar experiments can be run with a simple deck of cards, but playing cards have a great number of variables to consider when analyzing results. There is color, suit, and even the images that appear on face cards like the Kings and Queens. A sender may just pull a face card and start thinking about a living person. If the receiver records something too metaphorical, then it becomes much harder to judge the real accuracy of their "hit."

Researchers at the Maimonides Dream Institute ran into problems like this when running experiments involving works of art transmitted through dream telepathy. Several dreamers received images related to the artwork, but these were so interpretive that the data essentially had to be thrown out. The simplicity of the Zener cards is designed to make it much easier to identify a "hit" when one occurs.

Since their initial use in J.B. Rhine's experiments, the Zener cards have become something of a legend. There are online that detail their proper use in experiments, and there are even a few sites where you can participate in a simple Zener card experiment yourself. These sites, of course, are completely computer generated, nullifying the chance that your answers might be gleaned through telepathy, but precognition might still be measured through the use of such simple, computer-generated tests.

THE ETERNAL WARRIOR

The history books tell many tales about General George S. Patton Jr., for he was a colorful individual. From his exploits with the United States Tank Corps during WWI to his pentathlon competition in the 1912 Summer Olympics (where he swore he only lost first place because he neatly put one bullet through a hole left in the target by another!), to a rather infamous incident where he slapped two shell-shocked WWII soldiers in a misguided attempt to get them back into the fight, he left an impression wherever he went.

We know that Patton went to West Point, that he came from a military family, that he designed a unique type of calvary saber and even established rules for fencing not with foils but with broadswords. What we don't often hear with regards to "Old Guts and Glory" Patton are his beliefs in reincarnation.

While his family's military heritage undoubtedly played a role in his chosen profession, the man himself insisted that he was drawn to a life of soldiering because he had always been a warrior – and when he died, he would be reborn into a warrior's life again.

As a young man, Patton wrote a lengthy poem detailing what he believed were his various incarnations. Entitled, "Through a Glass, Darkly," the rhyming quatrains tell of lives that stretch into pre-history. He admits that he cannot name every battle, but gives details about fighting in a Phalanx against Cyrus and, later, fighting as a legionnaire in Rome. He claims to have died on Crécy's field during the 14th century conflict between England's Edward III and France's Philip VI, and to have held the rank of General as he galloped across the continent with Murat under Napoleon.

While the poem may be dismissed as a young man's fancy, there is a persistent tale told about Patton's time in Tunisia during WWII. The General was traveling by Jeep to an active battlefield. An increasingly intense and agitated Patton called out directions to his beleaguered driver, certain something important lay very near. Finally, they ended up near the Kasserine Pass, the site of a bloody massacre of one thousand American troops butchered in their first encounter with the German war-machine under Field Marshal Erwin Rommel. With the pass in the distance, Patton insisted that his driver stop.

The land around was empty, desolate. Patton got out and surveyed the field, finally satisfied. He then described a heated battle between the Carthaginians and three Roman legions that took place on that very spot. He insisted he had fought and died on that very battlefield ... in 146 BCE.

The Psychology of the Paranormal

Because paranormal and numinous experiences are marginalized in Western culture, those who experience them are often dismissed as crazy or delusional. Having been raised within the limits of Western culture, we ourselves often doubt the empirical evidence of our own direct experiences and struggle with the fear that we are simply insane. But what if I told you that one of the founders of modern psychology not only studied these abilities, but believed in them himself?

Carl Gustav Jung was an early student of Dr. Sigmund Freud and his work was influential to the evolving discipline of psychology. Later Freud's biggest rival, Jung is remembered as one of the fathers of modern psychology.

Although it is often swept under the rug, Jung was, in addition to his brilliant work in psychology and psychoanalysis, a mystic who studied Gnosticism and shamanism and who participated in seances very early in his career. His experiences with paranormal events in part inspired his theory of synchronicity. Writing in his book, *The Undiscovered Self,* this is what Jung himself had to say about the role of psychology in the science of the paranormal:

> "In the same way that our misconception of the solar system had to be freed from prejudice by Copernicus, the most strenuous efforts of a well-nigh revolutionary nature [are] needed to free psychology ... from the prejudice that the

psyche is, on the one hand, a mere epiphenomenon of a biochemical process in the brain or, on the other hand, a wholly unapproachable and recondite matter. The connection with the brain does not in itself prove that the psychic is an epiphenomenon, a secondary function causally dependent on biochemical processes ...

The phenomena of parapsychology ... warns us to be careful for they point to a relativization of space and time through psychic factors which casts doubt on our naive and overhasty explanation of the parallels between the psychic and the physical. For the sake of this explanation people deny the findings of parapsychology outright, either for philosophical reasons or from intellectual laziness. This can hardly be considered a scientifically responsible attitude, even though it is a popular way out of a quite extraordinary intellectual difficulty. To assess the psychic phenomenon, we have to take account of all the other phenomenon that come with it, and accordingly we can no longer practice any psychology that ignores the existence of the unconscious or of parapsychology.

The structure and physiology of the brain furnish no explanation of the psychic process. The psyche has a peculiar nature which cannot be reduced to anything else."

Notably, one of the core arguments that drove Jung and Freud apart revolved around Jung's mysticism. Freud felt psychology, if it were to be taken seriously as a science, had no room for paranormal beliefs. However, despite the hard stance Freud took against the paranormal throughout his early career, even he couldn't avoid it. He is widely known as the first person in modern times to document the phenomenon known as dream telepathy.

The Indubitable Charles Fort

He is the father of Fortean phenomenon – all of those events that defy the natural order as it is currently understood. Rains of frogs, invasions of previously undocumented insects, chunks of wood or other matter that mysteriously fall from the sky ... he documented everything, asking hard questions about what these events told us about the world in which he lived. He was Charles Fort, and his story is as intriguing as many of the events which he chronicled in his books.

Fort worked as a newspaper reporter in New York around the turn of the 20th century. Through this work, he became intrigued by stories of events that simply did not fit into the rational view that science applied to the world.

Fort himself took a view of extreme skepticism toward the world. He didn't believe in anything, least of all what he perceived to be the flimsy attempts made by science to present a neat and rational view of the world. He had a particular dislike for science, and he seemed to take perverse pleasure in knocking modern scientists down a few pegs by unearthing stories that threw a monkey wrench into their theories on physics, biology, and reality in general. For twenty-seven years, he poured over newspapers and journal articles, compiling stories of things that did not fit. He had little structure to his collections of these articles and his overall purpose seems to have been merely to present visions of the impossible and, through these visions, call into question the methods by which modern individuals tried to order the world.

Fort's research gave rise to a number of books, including his famous *Book of the Damned,* (1919) and

New Lands, (1923). In addition to his books that merely collected articles and reports of extraordinary and improbable experiences, Fort was also a prolific fiction writer. However, little of his fiction remains, as he was known to burn thousands of pages in fits of depression. He had the audacity to write his autobiography at the age of twenty-five, although even Fort himself, in later years, felt that this was presumptuous.

Through the work of his friend Tiffany Thayer, Fort's work was carried on after his death. Thayer founded the Fortean Society. The Fortean Society, as well as other Fort-inspired organizations and publications, continue to explore the edges of acceptable reality, presenting modern individuals with eye-witness accounts of strange and bizarre things that defy explanation.

THE BENTWATERS UFOS

They say that lightning never strikes in the same place twice, but that is not the case with UFOs. The Royal Airforce Base located at Lakenheath-Bentwaters in England was the site of two significant UFO encounters spaced almost exactly twenty-five years apart.

Witnesses at the NATO-affiliated air base reported the first incident in 1956. On the night of August 12th of that year, unidentified objects were spotted in the base's air space. The next night, things got really interesting. A transport pilot flying near the base reported seeing a number of lights in the sky. Controllers in the air tower at the Bentwaters base also observed these unidentified lights as they passed near their location. Base radar confirmed that something was in the skies that night, and it clocked the unidentified objects as flying at an astounding 2500 miles per hour.

This would have been extraordinary enough, but then a stationary object was sighted hovering just outside of the base. There was enough concern over this object that a Venom night-fighter jet was deployed to investigate. As the fighter jet approached it, the stationary object leapt into motion, rapidly accelerating to supersonic speeds. The UFO seemed to be taking evasive action, zipping here and there in the sky with the fighter jet struggling to keep up. The chase lasted for over thirty minutes, and before it was over, the UFO had turned the tables on the jet, whose pilot had to initiate some evasive maneuvers of his own to get the object off his tail. Running low on fuel, he landed, and a second jet was sent into the skies after the thing. This Venom fighter quickly developed instrument problems, however, and was rapidly grounded. The UFO left shortly afterward, as mysteriously as it had arrived.

As interesting as the night of August 13, 1956 proved to be at the Bentwaters base, the nights of December 26 and 27, 1980, were even more bizarre. The various reports connected with these winter nights have made the Bentwaters case famous among all the recorded incidents of British UFOs. A number of books of have been written about those nights, and although the British Office of Official Secrets has since released the only official written documentation of the Bentwaters UFOs, many UFOlogists insist that these documents were sanitized to obscure what really happened.

First, witnesses who lived near the Bentwaters base reported seeing lighted objects fall from the sky in the wee hours of December 26th. According to William Birnes' *UFO Encyclopedia*, British and American air traffic controllers in both civilian and military sites tracked these objects. The UFOs were headed in a trajectory toward Rendlesham Forest.

What happened next is a matter of some debate. The least conservative reports of the incident suggest that a UFO landed or crashed in the Rendlesham Forest, very close to the Bentwaters base. By some reports, base personnel made visible contact with extraterrestrials from the craft. The official documents released from the British Office of Official Secrets of course contains none of this. One thing is certain -- a number of people saw something in the skies on those cold nights immediately following Christmas, 1980. Perhaps the UFOs had returned to apologize for leading the Venom fighters in such a merry chase twenty-five years before.

Ancient Echoes of War

A Marathon is a 26-mile-long race that has been an integral part of the Olympic games since the 1896 games in Athens. But the race is also a part of both history and myth. In 490 BCE, a messenger was sent from the field of Marathon to Athens in order to report the Greek victory over the invading Persians. The messenger is said to have been a professional long-distance runner named Philippides who supposedly dropped dead in a typically heroic fashion immediately after completing his grueling run and, of course, delivering his important message. The news about the victory was of great importance to the city-state of Athens, and the historic Battle of Marathon was a key victory in the establishment of early Greek power.

In addition to its connection with long-distance running and Olympic games, the Battle of Marathon is one of the earliest recorded battles in history. The field saw an intense conflict unfold between the warriors of Athens and the invading force of Persia. Much like the American field of Gettysburg, the strength and intensity of the battle at Marathon may well have imprinted itself upon the surrounding countryside. Certainly, there are a number of historic reports that describe ghostly soldiers appearing at Marathon to relive the decisive battle. There are many reports about ghostly encounters in Greek and Roman literature, but the story of the Field of Marathon remains one of the most compelling.

Are the soldiers themselves somehow trapped in time, condemned to repeat this profound moment of their lives over and over again? Or are the ghostly combatants more akin to an echo that we can sometimes still hear, more than two thousand years later?

Some hauntings do not seem to be tied to sentient and free-willed beings, and haunted battlefields especially seem to fall into this category. Perhaps the strife and emotion inherent in the battle itself was enough to linger at the site of the bloodshed like a kind of psychic video-recording, playing and replaying for those with the capacity to sense it.

THE MYSTERY OF THE WATCHERS

"In those days, there were giants in the earth."

This passage, which opens Genesis 6:4 is one of the most compelling and mysterious statements in the Bible, and it has led to a great deal of speculation over the years, from debates about antediluvian bloodlines to hoaxes like the Cardiff Giant. The passage continues, growing even more peculiar, for it says,

> ...the sons of God came in unto the daughters of men, and they; bare children unto them, the same became mighty men which were of old, men of renown.

In some translations, the so-called "sons of God" are called the Nephilim. But who are the Nephilim, and what was their relationship with mankind in the early days of the Biblical world?

A lot of ink has been spilled over the issue of the Nephilim. The Bible itself says very little about them, mainly mentioning that they were attracted to the "daughters of men" and eventually took wives from among these beautiful daughters. But there is more to the story than the fragmentary passages that appear in Genesis. The *Book of Enoch* is a pseudepigraphal text written several hundred years before Christ's birth. It tells of a coming Messiah, and it further elaborates on the compelling story of the Watcher Angels, beings who expose the identity of the "sons of God" referenced in the Genesis passage.

The *Book of Enoch*, once viewed as sacred scripture by the early Church Fathers, was eventually cut out of accepted Biblical literature and lost to the world – until a version was rediscovered in Ethiopia by the famous explorer, James Bruce. The book tells of the Watcher Angels, Heavenly beings who were charged with the duty of watching over fledgling humanity. But the Watchers, led by the angels Shemyaza and Azazel, fell in love with their charges and reportedly walked out of Heaven in order to take up more human lives. They took wives from among the daughters of men, siring children and teaching their new families forbidden knowledge, such as root-cutting, astrology, and the art of cosmetics. The children of the Watchers were giants compared to their mortal mothers, and thus their existence gave rise to the Biblical notion of "giants in the earth." These half-angelic offspring were also called Nephilim, a word variously translated as meaning "the fallen ones" or, sometimes, "miscarriage" -- a supposed reference to the difficult births alleged to accompany the bearing of these giants.

According to the *Book of Enoch*, the sins of the Watchers, as well as the very existence of their half-angel sons, was the reason that the Flood was visited upon the earth. With the Flood, the progeny of the Watchers was cleansed from the earth, although certain Medieval legends attested that they remained in spirit-form to tempt and mislead mankind.

The story of the Watchers is both curious and compelling, and it has inspired a variety of interpretations. A number of UFOlogists see the Watchers as metaphors for alien beings who came down to interbreed with humanity. Their advanced knowledge led the people of the Biblical world to mistake them for gods or angels. Researcher Andrew Collins presents an alternate view. He sees the Watchers as the remnants of an earlier race, physically different enough from the people of the Biblical world to stand out as alien and even inhuman in their eyes. Although he never directly states it, Collins strongly implies that the Watchers may have been refugees from the lost Atlantis, or a similarly fallen civilization, whose advanced knowledge was perceived to have heavenly or supernatural origins.

Whatever the truth may be behind the Watchers and the Nephilim, the fragments that appear in Genesis and the curious story in the *Book of Enoch* both continue to pique the imagination, inspiring many writers and researchers to seek out the real meaning behind the mysterious giants and the otherworldly sons of God.

CHICAGO'S WHITE LADY

Tucked away in the trees near Rubio Woods Forest Preserve is Chicago's famous Bachelor's Grove Cemetery. A small one-acre graveyard with an ominous, weedy pond, Bachelor's Grove is probably the most haunted location in Chicago. Over one hundred reports of paranormal experiences have been recorded over the years.

The White Lady of Bachelor's Grove is the most common apparition. She appears on nights of the full moon. Her dress is white, and sometimes she carries a baby in her arms. Some have speculated that either she, or the baby, were drowned in the nearby lagoon. Other ghostly figures are sometimes seen rising from the waters of this eerie little pond. Some suspect that the Chicagoland gangs of the 1930s dumped bodies in the desolate little spot, secreting them in the murky waters of the pond. Others posit that the very location of the cemetery itself is haunted, and whatever strange power slumbers in the lagoon encourages the activities of the restless dead.

The best way to discover the truth is to explore for yourself. Bachelor's Grove is open to the public most days, typically closing at dusk. Located in Cook County in the southwest suburbs of Chicago, the cemetery is at 5900 W. Midlothian Turnpike, Midlothian, IL 60445. Parking is at Rubio Woods. The cemetery itself is across the street with an entrance to the right of the tower.

FIRE IN THE SKY

Most people associate UFOs with Roswell, New Mexico, where a crash allegedly took place in 1947. Thereafter, reports of unidentified flying objects proliferated, with significant clusters, or "flaps," of sightings occurring throughout the 1950s, 60s, and 70s.

To many, UFOs are a uniquely modern phenomenon, perhaps a kind of mass hallucination borne of collective anxieties surrounding the space-age. However, sightings of objects that seem identical to modern UFOs go back much, much further than 1947.

UFOlogist Jacques Vallée talks of an island in Hunan Province, China that has pre-historic carvings on a mountainside. The carvings have been tentatively dated to 45,000 BCE, placing them around the time of the Neanderthals. The carvings depict what are arguably spacecraft: a cluster of cylindrical objects flying through the sky.

Much controversy surrounds this interpretation of the prehistoric carvings in China. If UFO sightings can't be proven to go all the way back to the Neanderthals, they at least may stretch as far back as ancient Egypt. Another UFO writer, Brinsley Le Poer Trench, presents a passage from the annals of Pharaoh Thuthmose III in his 1966 book *The Flying Saucer Story*. This papyrus, written between 1504-1450 BCE tells of a peculiar phenomenon observed in the winter sky. The 3400-year-old text reads much like modern reports on UFO phenomenon. The scribe begins by giving specifics about the time and date of the initial sighting:

> In the year twenty-two, of the third month of winter, sixth hour of the day ...

The wording in the next section suggests that the scribes of the House of Life took the report, although they may not have been the ones who personally witnessed the first UFO:

> ... the scribes of the House of Life found it was a circle of fire that was coming in the sky ... It had no head; the breath of its mouth had a foul odor. Its body one rod long and one rod wide. It had no voice. Their hearts became confused through it; then they laid themselves on their bellies ...

But that would change. Apparently, the circular fires in the sky that plagued Egypt in the days of Thuthmose III were seen by a large number of individuals, including the Pharaoh himself:

> Now after some days had passed, these things became more numerous in the skies than ever. They shone more in the sky than the brightness of the sun, and extended to the limits of the four supports of the heavens ...
> The army of Pharaoh looked on with him in their midst. It was after supper. Thereupon, these fire circles ascended higher in the sky towards the south ...

The Pharaoh ordered the scribes of the House of Life to make a thorough search of their archives to see if anything of this nature had ever before been reported. As the current papyrus makes no mention that similar reports were found, perhaps this was Egypt's first. In the hope of staving off trouble, the Pharaoh ordered incense to be lit in order "to make peace on the hearth." Presumably it worked. The section concludes with Thuthmose III's final edict concerning the phenomenon:

> ...what happened was ordered by the Pharaoh to be written in the annals of the House of Life so that it be remembered forever.

Were these flying circles simply comets? Shooting stars? It's unlikely that the Egyptians of Thuthmose III's days would be confused about such aerial phenomena. The ancient Egyptians had a solid understanding of astronomy and made exacting observations of the movements of the sun, moon, planets, and stars. Many of their monuments, which stand to this day, were constructed to accurately align with numerous celestial events.

All we can say for certain is, thanks to Pharaoh Thuthmose III, a record of the flying fires in the sky has endured for thirty-four centuries.

Rapping with the Spirits

Every paranormal investigator should know the story of the Fox sisters, including Kate and Maggie, of Hydesville, New York. In 1848, the family provided the catalyst that ignited Spiritualism as a worldwide phenomenon. Young girls at that time (in Kate and Maggie's case, just 12 and 15 respectively), the sisters reported hearing a series of knocks and raps in their home which, ultimately, seemed to communicate intelligently with the girls to reveal a chilling tale of murder.

Similarly, every paranormal investigator should know that years later, the sisters recanted, revealing that all their spirit-communication claims were a hoax. We are told that Maggie and Kate both confessed to creating the rapping noises by popping the joints in their big toes, somehow deceiving all of the people who came to witness and investigate them.

And yet ... could there be more to the story?

The *Journal of the Society for Psychical Research*, volume IV, contains an interesting letter penned by one of the Fox sisters herself – Kate. Kate's letter is posted in the January 1889 edition.

The date is significant. It was only in November of 1888 that her sister Maggie Fox, at that point married as Maggie Kane, had rocked the world of Spiritualism by claiming everything the sisters had done had been faked. Shortly after this announcement, Maggie had gone on a lucrative tour, raking in thousands of dollars with her promoter, a professional skeptic who billed himself as "Professor" Star. Together with Star, who was a prestidigitator, Maggie claimed to reveal the chicanery behind her prior fame as a medium, making a kind of sideshow act out of it.

Reading further in the *Journal*, it becomes clear how little of this story has actually come down to the present day. If the letter from Kate Fox Jencken is genuine, then other lies were being told at the time, particularly by Maggie and Star. Kate claims that she was initially unaware of Maggie's claims of hoaxing, and Kate herself roundly denies that the spirit-communication they experienced was faked. It's important to note, however, that other articles written at the time place Kate with her sister on the hoax tour, fully in support of the exposure.

What was really going on?

In the interest of allowing people to judge for themselves, this article excerpts the entire entry from the *Journal of the Society for Psychical Research* (pp. 14-16) – not to argue authenticity or fraud, but to reveal the very human element that is present in the controversy on both sides.

Note that, at one point, Mrs. Jencken is debunked due to an unspecified "deplorable habit." I've not tracked down what this habit was just yet, although I suspect it might have involved spirits – the kind that come in a bottle. Of course, given the tenor of the times, a "deplorable habit" capable of wrecking public perception of a woman's moral rectitude could have been everything from smoking to consorting with unmarried men beyond the sight of her husband. The comment, put into perspective, would be rather like someone accusing a medium of being a fake because she posed for a swimsuit edition or had a habit of smoking marijuana.

Society for Psychical Research, Jan. 1889:

In the last number of the *Journal* there was a note on the confessions of the Fox sisters, Mrs. Kane and Mrs. Jencken. Since then a letter has been received from Mrs. Jencken by a friend of hers, in London and published in *Light*, in which her share in the alleged confession is – by implication though no expressly – denied. It seems only fair to Mrs. Jencken to print this letter here:

Letter from Mrs. Kate Fox Jencken
November 17th, 1888

"My dear Mrs. Cottell, – I would have written to you before this, but my surprise was so great on my arrival to hear of Maggie's exposure of Spiritualism that I had no heart to write to anyone.

The manager of the affair engaged the Academy of Music, the very largest place of entertainment in New York City; it was filled to overflowing. They made $1,500 clear. I have often wished I had remained with you, and if I had the means I would now return, to get out of all this.

I think now I could make money in proving that the knockings are *not* made with the toes. So many people come to me to ask about this exposure of Maggie's that I have to deny myself to them.

They are hard at work to expose the whole thing *if they can*; but they certainly cannot.

Maggie is giving public exposures in all the large places in America, but I have only seen her once since I arrived.

(signed) *K. F. Jencken*"

Our attribution to Mrs. Jencken of a share in the confession was based on the authority of several uncontradicted statements which had appeared in American journals. Among statements of this kind the following extract from the *Religio-Philosophical Journal* (a leading Spiritualistic paper in America), dated November 24th, 1888, may be read with interest in connection with Mrs. Jencken's letter:

Religio-Philosophical Journal:

On Thursday evening of last week [that is, November 15th, two days before the letter was written], at Rochester, NY, Mrs. Kate Fox Jencken joined forces with 'Professor' Star, who has for years made his living as an exposer of Spiritualism. Kate does not seem to have added much to the show, aside from the prestige of her presence.

We may note further that the news of Mrs. Jencken's co-operation with her sister in 'exposure' appears to have been unquestioningly accepted as true by the friends no less than the foes of Spiritualism in

England. The following paragraph, for instance, appeared in *Light* of November 3rd:

We learn from America that Mrs. Jencken and Mrs. Kane, two of the Fox sisters, have started on an exposure tour, in which they apparently propose to expose themselves first of all, and their dupes (if any) afterwards. It is always painful to be compelled to write of those whose names are familiar amongst us otherwise than in terms of commendation. But the issues at stake in Spiritualism are of wider import than the character of any individual. Painful, therefore, as it may be, we are compelled to say that no credence is to be attached to anything that these ladies may say. Mrs. Jencken has for a long time been a victim to a deplorable habit which has apparently destroyed her moral consciousness, and rendered anything she may say unworthy of attention.

As was said in the note that appeared in the *Journal* for December, little weight can be attached to what mediums who expose themselves may say, since they confess themselves deceivers; but in this case the confession seems to have been supported by experimental demonstration, and it would be strange on any hypothesis but that of trickery, that the raps should be capable of voluntary production for exposure purposes, and not capable of production when Professors Flint, Lee and Coventry, of Buffalo, in 1851, arranged the conditions so as to prevent the actions of the joints by which, in their opinion (founded on experiments with another person), they were caused. A brief account of their experiments condensed from Capron's *Modern Spiritualism*, published in 1856, will be found in *Proceedings*, vol. IV. p. 47.

Is there more to the Fox sisters' story? There was no Reality TV in 1888, but the controversy sounds all too familiar. There are echoes of exactly the same fears, criticisms, and accusations in paranormal community today. Within the community, we witness the making and breaking of alliances, gossip, fakery, bitter in-fighting, and slander, all stoked by money, fame, and competition.

Maybe some things will never change.

OAK ISLAND: DIGGING DEEPER

"Forty feet below two million pounds are buried."

The promise of buried treasure, believed to be contained in a strange cipher scribed upon a stone found in the Oak Island Money Pit has kept people digging through logs and clay and rising water for over two hundred years. But what is the Money Pit?

From the late 18th century onward, there has been a persistent belief that an island in Nova Scotia, Oak Island, to be exact, contains a secret. This secret has been theorized to be anything from pirate booty to the lost treasure of the Templars. The location of this secret is a small portion of land where, at one point, settlers discovered the block and tackle of a ship hanging from a tree. Beneath the block and tackle, there was a depression in the earth, and it seemed to logical to assume that something heavy enough to require the block and tackle had been, at some point, lowered into a pit, and that pit had been covered up to conceal this mysterious item. And so began the digging, as well as the legend of Oak Island.

Through the years, a variety of treasure (including a young Franklin Roosevelt!) have tried their hands at discovering what may have been placed into the pit. However, no matter how deep one digs, the Oak Island Money Pit seems to yield up only more puzzles and clues. The cipher, scribed upon a stone found at a depth of 90 feet, remains one of the most mysterious and most compelling. Comprised of simple geometric figures, most researchers accept the translation of this cipher as given above, and they see it as directions to the treasure that lies another forty feet below the point at which the cipher lay.

The problem with this, of course, has been the fact that, past a certain depth, the pit has begun to fill with water. Since diggers have had to work their way through seemingly endless layers of timber, clay, putty, and even coconut husks, the influx of water was seen as just another booby trap laid to prevent the discovery of the real treasure. But First Nations researcher Keith Ranville has recently proposed a new interpretation of the inscription, once which draws upon his knowledge of the pictograms of the Cree Salavics. Through his reassessment of the pictograms, Ranville asserts that the cipher actually details a complex tunnel system that connects Oak Island with the nearby Birch Island.

What might this network of tunnels really contain? Ranville prefers not to speculate. Considering that two hundred years of digging have failed to yield anything other than curious, compelling, and often frustrating clues, Oak Island may in fact contain nothing treasure-worthy at all. But the promise, and the mystery, keeps people digging still.

GREAT BALLS OF FIRE!

The lights are first visible just under the water. At first glance, you think they may be nothing more than reflections, perhaps some strange refraction of the moon overhead. And then the lights move with a life of their own, bursting out from beneath the surface of the river and rocketing like missiles toward the sky.

It sounds like a scene from some fantasy novel, but if you happen to be walking along the banks of the Mekong River in Thailand during the month of October, you may very well see this puzzling sight. The lights are attributed to the Mekong Dragon, a supernatural spirit of the river who governs the water flowing there. The Thai people propitiate this ancient being with a festival of lights. Dragon boats are raced upon the river, and human-made fireballs are launched into the sky in the form of cunningly crafted fireworks. But all of this pales to the amazing sight of the fireballs themselves, which emerge from the depths of the river and blaze forth in the night.

Are the lights man-made hoaxes? Perhaps they're merely swamp gas – although they would have to originate from some well-timed emissions, since the lights only emerge from the river during the time of the annual festival. Certainly, some strange things have come out of the Mekong River. Given the 646-pound catfish caught in 2005, the idea of a dragon lurking beneath those same waters becomes suddenly far more credible. Giant catfish aside, the river-born fireballs remain a mystery. While skeptics ponder, the Thai people engage in their lively festival, mingling Buddhist and animist beliefs in a richly textured worldview that leaves plenty of room for dragons.

WHERE LITTLE GREEN MEN COME FROM

On a hot August night in Kentucky, twelve people experienced an inexplicable night of terror in an isolated farm house. The place was Hopkinsville and the year was 1955. Five adults and seven children were staying in the house when, to their perception, an unidentified aircraft crashed in a nearby field. For the next several hours, the little farmhouse was under siege as apparent survivors swarmed outside the walls, peering into the windows and attempting to forcibly gain entry.

John Sutton and Billy Ray Taylor, two of the adult occupants, fended the invaders off with a pistol and shotgun. When they finally felt safe enough to venture out, they approached the police with their harrowing tale.

At the station, they described beings small in stature with long arms and webbed, clawed hands. They had pointed ears and widely-spaced, glassy eyes that shone brightly in the shadows. None of the witnesses specifically described the color of the little creatures' skin in their initial interviews, but somehow the idea that they were green was taken up by the press. Soon newspaper outlets all over the country featured articles debating the identity of the "little green men." Others called them goblins, and so the legend of the Hopkinsville goblins was born.

After taking the harried peoples' reports, the local police investigated. Although they found ample evidence of the discharge of firearms from inside the house, no tracks or other signs of a physical presence around the farmhouse could be found. There was also no sign of a crashed UFO, although one of the Hopkinsville police officers remembered having seen a meteor shower in the area that same night.

Given the sheer number of people who claimed to have witnesses these little beings – and not fleetingly, but over the course of several hours – it was hard to entirely dismiss the event. But were the creatures aliens? Goblins? Something stranger still?

Those who dismiss the incident claim that the meteor shower spooked the family and, fueled by alcohol, they began shooting at things that weren't there. Others suggest that they mistook owls for the little aliens, and certainly, owlets could pass for enormous-eyed aliens in the wrong light. After the initial Hopkinsville report, there was a wave of similar sightings, including one from a group of teens from Evansville, a town about eighty miles north. These youngsters claimed to have encountered nearly a dozen of the creatures in the Lincoln High School athletic field. They were driven off when the teens started throwing rocks.

Fever Dreams

Lord Byron rocketed to fame with the publication of his autobiographical poem, *Childe Harold's Pilgrimage*, in 1812. He became an instant sensation in his native England, but his skills as a poet only played a part in his fame. Byron was a mysterious figure, renowned for his brooding and melancholy, and his beliefs and actions both fascinated and repulsed many of his admirers.

Born with a clubbed foot, he often played up the notion that the Devil shared the same deformity. In his writings, he variously identified himself with Lucifer, Cain, Shemyaza, and Faust. At his haunted ancestral home of Newstead Abbey, he was rumored to run Black Masses. Although there is no proof that Byron practiced Satanism in any serious way, we do know that he had an old skull crafted into a chalice so he could drink wine from this grisly cup.

Byron was someone who knew how to play to his fame, and he had fun building upon his natural aura of mystery. But, from at least a few reports, it is possible that there was more to Byron's involvement with the supernatural than mere show. A report by the distinguished person of Sir James Peel suggests that Byron possessed the power of bilocation.

In 1810, Peel met Byron on the street and held a brief conversation with the poet. At the time, however, Byron was nowhere near England. His physical body lay in Patras, Greece, desperately ill with a fever. Did the fever enable Byron somehow to astrally project? If so, he was able to produce such a solid phantom that Peel mistook it for the real thing.

NINE TENTHS OF THE LAW

A Capuchin, a Franciscan, and Jesuit go to an exorcism ...

It sounds like the beginning of a bad joke, but in seventeenth century France it was a deadly serious business for Urbain Grandier. Grandier was a parish priest in Loudun, France, accused of sending demons to possess a convent of Ursuline nuns. A worldly priest, Grandier was tall and attractive with a reputation for not exactly upholding his vow of celibacy to the letter. He had made a lot of enemies both through his sexual indiscretions and his political leanings. In 1618, he penned a sarcastic little piece criticizing Cardinal Richelieu.

Richelieu was not a man easily trifled with, and he was to become one of the most powerful political figures in France at the time. Known for his skills at intrigue and subterfuge, Richelieu may very well have been the driving force behind a scheme to destroy Grandier, using the wide-spread belief in demons and witchcraft to shatter Urbain's reputation.

In 1630, a group of Ursuline nuns accused Grandier of summoning demons to torment and possess them. To prove this, they went into convulsions and threw wild fits, often performing lewd acts and exposing themselves in a demonically-inspired frenzy. One of Grandier's many enemies, a Father Mignon, undertook the task of exorcising the nuns. His work produced a number of curious documents, allegedly written by the demons in possession of the nuns. Asmodeus, writing in bad French in a delicate woman's hand, apparently penned a contract promising to leave the body of the nun in his possession.

Later, when Grandier's case came to trial, this would be submitted as evidence against him. A contract was similarly penned, alleged to be Grandier's pact with the Devil. It is countersigned by a variety of well-known demons, including Baalberith, Astaroth, and Beelzebub. This document also was later produced as evidence in Grandier's trial.

Mignon's efforts at exorcism seemed only to encourage the nuns, and eventually he was forbidden to continue with his work. However, Grandier continued to be a thorn in the side of Cardinal Richelieu. Before the whole thing was over, the Cardinal got directly involved in the Loudun case, ordering a full investigation and setting aside funds to hire further exorcists. Cue the Capuchin, the Franciscan, and the Jesuit, who all engaged in dramatic and zealous public displays of exorcising the nuns. The entire event became a spectacle, and as the public heard accusation after accusation coming from the mouths of the supposedly possessed nuns, the people of Loudun began to suspect that Grandier had indeed signed a pact with the Devil.

Grandier was arrested, and Richelieu himself took control of the proceedings. The French Cardinal was not one to forgive an insult, and thus things did not go well for Grandier. He was tortured horribly and then burned at the stake for witchcraft in 1634. The entire case is grippingly recounted in Aldous Huxley's intriguing work, *The Devils of Loudun*.

The nuns continued to behave as though possessed even after Grandier's death. Richelieu was the only member of the clergy able to finally drive the devils out of them. He threatened to cut off their funding if they did not cease and desist.

THE BELL WITCH

Among the many famous American hauntings is the Bell Witch of Tennessee. Often classed as a poltergeist despite its witchy identifier, this is a haunting that has achieved near-legendary status. Reputed to have occurred in the early 1800s, the Bell Witch legend revolves around a curse alleged to have afflicted John Bell and his family. The curse was pronounced by his neighbor Kate Batts, a woman who claimed till her dying breath that John Bell had cheated her in a sale of some land – and she would have her revenge.

Volume five of the *American Historical Magazine* (1900) tells us, "From 1818 to 1835 the stories of the Bell Witch created great excitement in Robertson County, and throughout Middle Tennessee." Of course, like most legends, the Bell Witch has very little in the way of documentation beyond the anecdotal reports of the locals. Almost everything that survives related to the case involves second and third-hand reports. But those reports are nevertheless interesting.

In a recent search for primary materials related to the Bell Witch haunting, I turned up an entry in *Tennessee: A Guide to the State*. Part of the *American Guide Series*, this was compiled by the Federal Writers' Project and published by Viking Press in 1939 – long after both Kate Batts and John Bell were dust in their graves. Although it is hardly a primary material, the entry is still one of the oldest surviving articles on the Bell Witch I've yet been able to dig up and read in completion.

It tells an interesting tale. Here is the full entry from pages 392-393 of the *Tennessee State Guide* so you can see for yourself:

The Bell Witch Farm
"The Bell Witch Farm has long been so called because it is widely believed that a witch hag rode John Bell and his family here during the early part of the nineteenth century. At the turn of the century John Bell came to Tennessee from North Carolina, bought a tract of land here and settled with his large family and numerous slaves. To round out his holdings, Bell bought a section of land from Mrs. Kate Batts, a neighbor who had a reputation for meanness. Bell was noted for an almost grim piety and uprightness; yet no sooner had the land transfer been complete than Mrs. Batts began declaring that Bell had cheated her. This fancied injustice vexed the old woman for years. On her deathbed she swore that she would come back and 'hant John Bell and all his kith and kin to their graves.'

Sure enough, tradition says, the Bells were tormented for years by the malicious spirit of Old Kate Batts. John Bell and his favorite daughter Betsy were the principal targets. Toward the other members of the family the witch was either indifferent or, as in the case of Mrs. Bell, friendly. No one ever saw her, but every visitor to the Bell home heard her all too well. Her voice, according to one person who heard it, 'spoke at a nerve-racking pitch when displeased, while at other times it sang and spoke in low musical tones.'

The spirit of Old Kate led John and Betsy Bell a merry chase. She threw furniture and dishes at them. She pulled their noses, yanked their hair, poked needles into them. She yelled all night to keep them from sleeping, and snatched food from their mouths at mealtime.

The witch, so they say, did not confine her capers to the Bell farmstead. She attended every revival in Robertson County and outsang, outshouted, outmoaned the most fervent converts. The unseen Kate was also very fond of corn whisky. She constantly raided stillhouses, they say, got roaring drunk, and went home to belabor John and Betsy Bell with renewed fervor.

When Betsy fell in love with Josiah Gardener, a young man who lived on the adjoining farm, Old Kate included Josiah in her vigorous displeasure. Gardener finally gave up and fled from the State.

When Old Kate's fame at length reached Nashville, Andrew Jackson and some friends determined to face the terror and 'lay' it once and for all. In very high spirits they set out for the Bell farm. Suddenly, on the boundary of Bell's property, it is related, the wagon in which Jackson and his friend were riding would move no farther. The mules strained and Jackson cursed. Out of the empty air came Kate's voice: 'All right, General, the wagon can move on.' And it did.

That night Kate kept the house in an uproar. She sang, she swore, she threw dishes, overturned furniture, and snatched the bedclothes from all the beds. Next morning, the harried Jackson made an early start, crying out to Bell as he left, 'I'd rather fight the British again than have any more dealings with that torment.'

The Bell Witch disappeared when John Bell died. The original farmhouse has been torn down. At intervals the newspapers revive the story with an account of how some descendent of Bell's is due for a visitation, which they say is the lot of one person in each generation."

Most of the information in the entry seems to have been taken from a publication by one of the Bell descendants, Charles Bailey Bell. A neurologist from Nashville, his own book, *The Bell Witch, a Mysterious Spirit*, was printed by the Lark Bindery in 1934, supposedly one year before Old Kate's prophesied return. Prior to his work, the earliest publication referenced is *An Authenticated History of the Famous Bell Witch: The Mysterious Talking Goblin That Terrorized the West End of Robertson County, Tennessee*, by Martin V. Ingram. This was published in Clarksville by W.P. Titus in 1894, -- but no copies of the text itself seem to have survived the decades.

For those curious about this famous American haunting, more can be found in *Studies in Philology*, Vol 16, 1919, starting on page 237. In this report, based on Ingram's currently lost-to-us book, there are indications that the "witch" had an interesting power to appear in the form of animals. It manifested as something like a dog to

Mr. Bell and, on another occasion, his son Drew saw the witch take the form of something akin to a turkey. One of Mr. Bell's slaves, a man named Dean, claimed to have seen the spirit in the guise of a large black dog. Betsy and the children saw it as a little girl dressed in green once, and on other occasions, it took the form of a hare.

Notably, only a few other poltergeist cases include reports of strange animals appearing in association with the destructive spirit. Primary among these is a visitation reported on the Isle of Man in the 1930s in which the spirit identified as a poltergeist was reputed to appear as a small talking animal, reminiscent of a mongoose. This strange and mischievous little being declared its name to be Gef, and tales of Gef the Talking Mongoose are familiar on the Isle of Man to this day.

Call Him Corpsedancer

In the popular folklore of Europe, demons and the spirits of the damned were associated with places of execution. Sometimes they were also associated with the physical remains of the murderers and thieves themselves. Normally, this association resulted in rumors that witches and necromancers made use of the bodies of executed criminals as components of their spells. At least one spell in the *Liber de Angelis* calls for the magician to go to a place of execution in order to call up the dark spirits of a curse. But nowhere is the connection between demons and the gallows quite so pronounced as in the story of Nicole Aubri.

Nicole Aubri was a young woman native to Vervins, in France. In an account recorded by the eighteenth-century folklorist and theologian, Dom Augustin Calmet, this poor woman came to the attention of the demon Baltazo.

Baltazo had amorous intentions toward Nicole, but she was a married woman and repeatedly spurned his advances. As part of his infernal courtship, the demon purportedly took possession of the body of a hanged man who then stepped down from his gibbet and accosted Nicole's husband. The demon demanded the right to pass a night with the poor woman while clothed in this grisly form. In return for one night in her conjugal bed, the demon promised to leave Nicole alone for the rest of her life. The husband, certain of the demon's treachery, declined this dubious offer.

NIGHTMARE IN THE SKIES

Precognition is the psychic ability to gain glimpses of the future – often in the form of prophetic dreams. Most instances of precognition are difficult to verify, mainly because the dream is a one-time event and the experiencer fails to write the details down until after the foreseen event has transpired. More rarely still are precognitive dreams taken seriously by authorities, which typically leads to silence among those who have these nightly visions: they never expect to be taken seriously, so they keep their experiences to themselves.

This was not the case for David Booth, a twenty-three-year-old living in Cincinnati, Ohio. In 1979, Booth worked as an office manager by day, but his nights were plagued with a recurring nightmare. Every time he lay down to sleep, he ended up watching a deadly plane crash at an airport. First, he heard the sound of engines failing, then he saw the plane swerve and roll in the sky. Finally, it plunged, inverted, to the tarmac, a wreck of metal and flame. He could even see the company logo: American Airlines.

Certain that this was no mere night terror – and that the crash would come soon – Booth made several calls on Tuesday, May 22, 1979. If there were a way he could prevent this tragedy, he felt obligated to try it, even if he ended up sounding crazy. Just in case, however, one of his calls was to a psychiatrist. But he also called American Airlines and the Federal Aviation Administration at the Greater Cincinnati International Airport. He hoped he would be taken seriously.

In most cases of precognitive dreams, when (or if) the dreamer reaches out with their warning, no one believes. This is the Cassandra Effect, named for the ill-fated princess of Troy in Greek myth who foresaw the fall of that great city but whose warnings were universally ignored.

In Booth's case, however, he had so many compelling details in the dream that the Federal Aviation Administration actually paid attention. As was later explained by Jack Barker, the public affairs officer representing the FAA's southern region, they scoured their available information, trying to match what Booth was seeing to potential flights. The plane he described strongly suggested that the crash would involve a DC-10. They had the airline, and they even had some details of the airport and its runways where the crash would occur.

But they couldn't put the pieces together in time.

A few days later, on May 25th, at Chicago O'Hare International Airport, American Airlines Flight 191, bound for Los Angeles, lost an engine just after take-off. The plane faltered, rolling in the air. It crashed, inverted, onto the runway in a fiery explosion that killed all two-hundred and seventy-seven people on board. At the time, it was the deadliest airline disaster the US had ever experienced.

Each detail of the crash matched David Booth's unnerving dream, down to the make of the aircraft: it was a DC-10.

AMERICAN VAMPIRES

If you keep up with American vampire lore, you have almost certainly heard about the case of Mercy Brown. Mercy, as resident of Exeter, Rhode Island, was one of several family members to succumb to tuberculosis – an affliction known in those days as consumption. Mercy's mother, Mary Eliza, had been the first to die, and she was followed in 1886 by her oldest daughter, Mary Olive. Mercy and her brother Edwin both contracted the disease. Mercy died on January 17, 1892. By this point, rumors abounded that someone in the family was a vampire and they were afflicting the other Browns from beyond the grave. This was a common superstition of the day, tied up with poorly understood mechanics of contagion and corruption.

On March 17, 1892, the fears of the remaining family members had grown so extreme that they consented to have Mary Eliza, Mary Olive, and Mercy all exhumed and examined for signs of vampirism. The sign everyone was looking for involved a lack of decay in the corpse. As the belief in vampires went at the time, the life-force being stolen from the remaining living family went to support the corpse in the grave. This fended off the natural process of decomposition.

When the three deceased members of the Brown family were exhumed, both Mary Eliza and Mary Olive were found to have what onlookers deemed "natural" signs of decay. Mercy, however, did not. Accordingly, her heart and liver were removed and burned. The ashes were then used in a tonic and given to Edwin to drink. It was believed that, by drinking this grisly concoction, he would stave off the vampire and be cured.

He died two months later.

As strange an episode as the Mercy Brown case might seem, it was by no means an isolated incident at the time. Moncure Daniel Conway, writing in *Demonology and Devil-Lore* (1879) tells of one Dr. Dyer of Chicago, Illinois who reported on an 1875 case of vampirism in that city. The details are almost identical to the Mercy Brown case: family members were dying of consumption, one of the earliest to have succumbed was accused of being a vampire. The family believed that member, unchecked, would bring all the rest with them to the grave. Accordingly, the corpse was exhumed and mutilated. In this case, only the lungs were burned and used in the cure.

Based on Conway's information, Mercy Brown was only one in a long line of Rhode Island vampires exhumed to keep other family members alive. In 1874, a family with the last name of Rose had a similar outbreak. They lived in Peacedale, Rhode Island, and, like Mercy, it was their daughter who fell under suspicion of being a vampire. The *Providence Journal* recounted the sad tale, which ended once more with exhumation, mutilation, and a desperate, stomach-churning attempt at a cure.

ALL HALLOWS' HAGS

In the US, we dress up for Halloween. Children run around begging for candy threatening "tricks" if they don't get their "treats." Originally imported with Irish immigrants, Halloween, or All Hallows' Eve, is a celebration that takes place one night before the Catholic Feast of All Souls. Fully secularized and commercialized since then, Halloween has evolved into a uniquely American holiday. But the Irish were not the only people of the British Isles to practice all Hallows' traditions before Halloween came to America.

In Wales, specifically in the vicinity of Llanfyllin, there used to be an old custom for the working men to dress themselves in sheeps' skins and ragged old clothes on All Hallows' night. The practice is recounted on page 79 of the 1891 publication, *Bye-gones: relating to Wales and the border countries.* The men would mask their faces and take to the streets, going from house to house, stopping at the public houses, where they drank for free during the celebration. The whole night was one of rowdy carousing and begging, and people would give coppers, apples, and nuts.

These All-Hallows' revelers were called *Gwrachod*, or hags. The tradition stemmed from a belief among the Celts that "fiends, witches, and fairies are thought to be all abroad on their baleful errands during this night." Since the revelers were working men and not children, the celebration could get out of hand, leading to tussles and destruction of property. Eventually the practice was put down by the police.

The Work of the Devil

In the Middle Ages, the Devil seemed to be everywhere in Europe. If one credits the witch craze, Satan himself spent a great deal of time touring the countryside and seducing hapless old women into flying off with him to have wild orgies in the woods. Through a liberal application of torture, witch-finders would pull colorful, elaborate, and wholly incredible confessions from suspected witches, and many of these detailed the varied and devious ways in which the Devil and his many demons sought to corrupt and obtain human souls.

According to some folklore, however, demons weren't always a nuisance to humanity. Occasionally, the Devil, or one of his cohorts, could be put to productive use. Grillot de Givry, in his lavishly illustrated collection, *Witchcraft, Magic and Alchemy*, recounts a number of tales that attribute feats of great industry to demonic beings. A variety of bridges and other building projects were supposedly constructed with the help of the Devil. His traditional payment? Old Nick would request the soul of the first living being to make use of his work.

Wily villagers would apparently take the Devil's help, but then find a way to trick him of his due. This gave rise to the tale of the Wolf's Door at the cathedral in Aachen, Germany, where a wolf was supposedly driven into the new cathedral upon its inauguration, so that this wild beast could fall prey to the Devil in place of some righteous soul. A similar folk belief is recorded in the stained glass at the old church in St. Cado, France. Here, the Devil finished construction on a local bridge, and requested the soul of the first living being to walk across. St. Cado came on the day that the bridge was finished and released a cat, cheating the Devil.

One of the most interesting versions on this theme of the Devil's work is connected with nothing less than the grand cathedral of Notre Dame de Paris. During the construction of the great cathedral (as the story goes) a journeyman ironworker was given the task of producing the ironwork for the doors to Notre Dame. This work was to be his test-piece for admission to his guild, but he soon found that the work was too much for him. Each door was an immense twenty-two feet by thirteen feet, and he was expected to decorate this entire expanse.

Enter the demon Biscornet. He offered to produce cunningly beautiful ironwork over all of the doors in exchange for the journeyman's soul. Desperate to complete his task, the journeyman agreed. The next morning, four doors for the right and left doorways were completed, and the ironwork was amazing to behold. There wasn't even a visible seam. However, Biscornet could not complete the work on the middle doors because these would see the passage of the Holy Sacrament during processions. Since Biscornet could not finish the task, the journeyman got to keep his soul – as well as the four completed doors. These were up on the cathedral for all to see until Viollet-le-Duc's restoration of the cathedral in 1860.

The current doors are a faithful reproduction of Biscornet's work, although they lack the inhuman perfection of the previous pieces of ironwork.

M. Belanger

COME HAVE A BALL AT MYRTLE HILL

If you live near Medina County, Ohio, chances are, you've heard about the Witch's Ball. It's not a dance nor a swanky Halloween party. Medina County's Witch's Ball is a grave.

The ball is located in an out-of-the-way cemetery called Myrtle Hill, which also boasts proximity to Cry Baby Bridge on Abbeyville Road, another allegedly haunted location surrounded by local legends. The cemetery is off the beaten path, and, although a number of houses have started to encroach upon it in recent years, it's still fairly remote, surrounded by open fields and woods.

A lot of locals frequent the Witch's Ball, especially around Halloween. As the story goes, a witch is buried under the striking, spherical monument emblazoned with the name Stoskopf. The witch, for one reason or another (the reasons vary depending on which version of the legend you happen to hear), still lingers near her earthly remains, and she is not at all happy to be there. Allegedly, the huge granite sphere perched on top of her monument thrums with powerful energy. Cold in summer, warm in winter, to place your hands upon the Witch's Ball and feel the temperature of the stone suddenly change is considered a bad omen indeed.

One of the more elaborate local legends that has grown up around this unusual monument is that the witch was one of three sisters, all buried in the area in graves marked with some manner of sphere. The three graves are arranged along ley lines, and they describe a triangle that marks a place of dark energy.

This author, who grew up not far from Myrtle Hill, has been out at night to lay hands upon the fabled ball. Friends have sought the other two graves, to no avail. The ley line myth is likely just that, and a little research reveals that, despite the reputation of the Stoskopf grave, a man, and not a woman, is buried there.

Despite this, legends persist about the grave. Paranormal researcher Nick Reiter of the Avalon Foundation looked into the myth of the Witch's Ball in the late 1990s. Although no angry witch leapt out of the shadows to attack or curse him, he did learn that the huge granite sphere has what amounts to an electromagnetic pulse. Upon close inspection of the monument, the granite is revealed to have a high quartz content, and Nick theorized that at least some of the strange sensations experienced by those laying their hands upon the gravestone are legit. However, rather than arising from the failing powers of a dead witch, Reiter believes that a natural geode exists within the stone. This collection of quartz crystals, combined with the size and shape of the stone, seems to conduct a small but perceptible amount of energy throughout, which he recorded on his instruments.

Telepathic Theory of Apparitions

Would it seem strange to you, dear reader, if I said that -- at least at one point in the history of paranormal research -- it seemed more plausible to some investigators to explain ghostly apparitions based on the action of human telepathy rather than allow for the possibility of the spirit's survival after death?

Curious? Here's a letter to the editor from the *Journal of the Society for Psychical Research* from the November 1889 issue. Written by a Samuel Joyce, Junior, the letter professes to explain so-called "Phantasms of the Dead," i.e., apparitions of spirits, through the mechanism of telepathy or thought-transference.

As you read the portions of this letter to the editor excerpted below, consider how telepathy is presented as an almost inarguable truth while, at the same time, the author strives to debunk the notion of spirits and the survival of the personality after death.

It's not my purpose here to take sides on the matter, but instead to raise questions about this particular writer's logic – and what that logic tells us about the beliefs of his times. From the tone of his letter, and the fact that it got published in the SPR's *Journal*, it seems safe to assume that the Society did not dismiss him out of hand as a crackpot – some merit must have been seen to his argument, otherwise it would never have seen print. But this means that there was a much stronger belief in the existence of telepathy among the members of the SPR than there might have been a belief in ghosts, which is curious unto itself. Consider the state of paranormal investigation now, a little more than a hundred years later. What are our broadly-stated stances on the existence of telepathy versus that of spirits? How have attitudes changed – and, more importantly, why?

I'll let you ponder these questions as you read through Mr. Joyce's intriguing letter on the telepathic explanation of apparitions.*

*I have presented this letter unaltered save for one small thing: I have created some breaks in large blocks of text to facilitate reading in an electronic format.

A Theory of "Haunting"
Letter to the Editor of the *Journal of the Society for Psychical Research*
pp. 165-168 Nov. 1889

In investigating the subject of apparitions, the Society for Psychical Research have named one class "Phantasms of the Living," being cases of the appearance to friends or relations of persons at or near the moment of death. These have been very successfully dealt with on the telepathic theory, and it is my object to extend that theory so as to embrace the cases of Phantasms of the Dead. This has, indeed, been done to a certain extent already, but there are many points to be explained.

In her paper on "Phantasms of the Dead" in Part VIII of the *Proceedings of the Society for Psychical Research*, Mrs. Sidgwick gives four theories of apparitions. The first two require the agency, through practically unlimited time, of either the mind of the disembodied spirit, or of the quasi-physical spirit itself; but, however much we may believe in the mental activity of a person when dying, we have no right to assume continued activity after the cessation of all that we really know of as individual personality. The third and fourth theories I would combine, as I believe together they will give – especially if extended – a working hypothesis for the examination of new cases.

These two theories are that the first appearance is not due to the dead at all but is a purely subjective hallucination on the part of the percipient; and subsequent appearances are, on the part of the first percipient, due to unconscious expectancy; and on the part of others due to "some sort of telepathic communication from the first percipient." Also, that "some subtle physical influence" in certain buildings may be the cause of an apparition. I would extend and modify these two theories into one, viz: The first appearance may be due to the telepathic transference of a mental effort on the part of some person *not necessarily* the decedent or even a relation of the decedent. Subsequent appearances may be due to the same cause, or to the mental effort of the first percipient as a new source of telepathic disturbance.

The telepathic impressions may be the more easily perceived or appreciated by the percipient when helped by various external physical coincidences, e.g., a view of the actual room may help the perception of the event thought of as being enacted therein.

When considered in all its bearings this last point will be found to have a wide range of application. It entirely does away with the necessity of a so-called localization (sic) of telepathic impressions -- though this may very possibly exist. For, if we suppose a telepathic disturbance set up by some agent at a centre, to be otherwise equally perceptible along all radii from that centre, it will be quite reasonable to suppose that that percipient who is, as it were, helped to the perception of the mental picture by the actual perception of a real and physical part of it will be the most likely -- perhaps the only -- one to receive any abnormal impression.

It will be seen that the main departures from Mrs. Sidgwick's theories are that the centre of telepathic disturbance may be someone quite other than the decedent or even a relation to the decedent; and that the "subtle physical influence" is reduced to nothing more remarkable than something similar to the help which the sight of a familiar room or place may be able to afford as a reminder of an event which took place in that room or place.

It will, perhaps, make matters clearer if I review some cases from the Society's collection in the light of the foregoing remarks. Take the case published in the *Proceedings*, Vol. I., p. 108. This is an account of the repeated apparition through a long period of time of a lady who was considered by various percipients to be friendly towards them though quite unconnected with their concerns. The lady who is supposed to be the original of this ghost was a Miss A., and seems to have met with a tragic end. Did she die unmarried, leaving a disconsolate lover behind, in whose thoughts she ever dwelt? Such a mental picture on the part of the lover would be, on my theory, easily perceived by those who were sensitive and dwelt in and about the house -- which would be most likely the actual scene of the mental picture.

Again, there is a case given in the *Proceedings*, Vol. V., p. 415. A lady who used to live in the country dies in London, and is seen by a stranger on the same day walking round a tomb, which she appears to have often visited when living in the country. May not the percipient have realised (sic) the telepathic impression received from some friend of relation of decedent, who upon hearing of the death thought naturally of the decedent as performing a favourite act, especially when such impression was helped into being by the actual sight of the tomb in question. This seems the more natural since the appearance was not for some hours after the actual death.

In the discussion of this case in the paper above cited, the following remarks are made: "It certainly tells, as far as a single case can tell, in favour of the theory of independent *post-mortem* appearance as opposed to that of telepathy, or thought-transference, in the ordinary sense. For on the one hand the hypothesis of a transferred impression from the mind of a dying person seems strained to the uttermost when (as in this case) the dying person and the percipient have been connected by no tie of blood or friendship."

This seems to imply that thought-transference only or mainly takes place between persons related by blood, or close friends; but I think we have no warrant for this conclusion, and there are many other cases in which the percipient was a stranger ...

This complete telepathic theory seems on the first impression to involve a much more extended sensibility to telepathic impression than we have hitherto seen ground for supposing. But when we think that all or most of our thought-transference experiments have been conducted with such comparatively uninteresting objects for mental concentration on the part of the agent, as a card, a number, or a simple geometrical figure, and without any aid to the right interpretation of the mental impression on the part of the percipient, and have, nevertheless, often succeeded; how much more should we expect success in the case of one person out of the millions who are supposed to be within the range of the telepathic influence, when the subject for mental concentration on the part of the agent is of such an intensely interesting and soul-absorbing nature as the contemplation of the form of a deceased loved relation; especially when there is the external physical aid to the interpretation afforded by the actual view of the room, building, or place which the agent has in mind ..."

Does it take more mental gymnastics to explain away ghosts as telepathic projections? Or are there too many theological complications to accepting the survival of the soul after physical death?

Perhaps instead there are multiple explanations for the variety of ghostly encounters, including intelligent spirits, residual hauntings, and psychic projections. The best way for paranormal enthusiasts to find out is to keep investigating.

What's Your Color?

According to many psychics and energy workers, each and every human being is surrounded by a nimbus of light. This full-body halo is the human aura, and it is believed to be the extension of our personal energy fields. Some claim to be able to see the aura, describing it most often in terms of light and color. Still others claim to have invented gadgets that can photograph this otherworldly glow so you can own a picture of your own aura for $19.95 -- and sometimes, considerably more.

There are a baffling number of aura cameras out there, and they claim to reveal everything from potential health problems to a person's current mood. If you're shopping for a camera that will just let you point and click and get an image of your aura, however, you might find the market a little thin. Most aura cameras out there don't actually photograph the energy field around a person. Instead, they rely on principles of bio-feedback and galvanic skin response to compile the image of a *probable* aura, and then they project this onto a photo or other image for the curious to see.

There's the Aura Spectrophotometer 5200, that claims to measure the frequencies of a person's bio-magnetic field through the use of sensors embedded in handplates. The system then takes the data gleaned from these sensors and essentially designs an appropriately colored aura around an image of the person. Then there's the Inneractive Aura Video Station that uses a similar handplate, or biosensor, but then allows you to view your aura in real-time. Palm-focused sensors are also integral to the function of the Aurastar 2000 as well as its high-tech successor, the Biopulsar-Reflexograph. The names sure sound impressive, don't they?

This author had the opportunity to give the Aurastar 2000 a whirl several years ago at a local psychic fair. Like a lot of people, I was disappointed at first to learn that the so-called aura camera wasn't really photographing anything at all. But the image the Aurastar 2000 did spit out looked interesting enough, and one of the operators offered an interpretation of the colors that nailed a few personal details right on the head. In the end, I had a colorful image to commemorate the event, but I remained skeptical of the "science" involved in procuring it.

If aura cameras aren't taking photos of a person's aura, what (if anything) are they tuning in on? CSICOP skeptic Joe Nickell, believes the devices might be tuning in to the electromagnetic activity of the nerves or even the weak sonic and chemical emissions the human body. It's unlikely that such emissions could reveal the true nature of a person's spirit guides, but insight into a person's health and well-being remains within the realm of possibility. All in all, the technology of aura photography can be as fuzzy as some of its photos but, it remains one of the only methods around for trying to compile an image of the human energy field so many psychics claim to see.

THE WAY OF THE SECRET MASTERS

Founded in New York in 1875, the Theosophical Society dedicated itself to the exploration of mediumship and its many applications and powers. At the time, the phenomenon of mediumship had become more than a passing fancy in both America and England. This was thanks in no small part to the strange occurrences at the Hydesville, New York home of the Fox sisters in 1848. The Theosophical Society promoted the study of what they called *theosophy*, which essentially means "knowledge of God."

Headed by the charismatic and controversial figure of Helena Petrovna Blavatsky, the society started off with fairly simple goals. After a few years, however, the headquarters of the society were moved from New York to Madras, India -- a locale which, at the time, must have seemed exceptionally exotic to most Westerners.

The move to Madras reflected one of Blavatsky's great passions, a passion which was to have a hefty impact upon the beliefs and goals of the society. In a time when Imperialism was grinding the country of India underfoot, Blavatsky was looking at Hindu culture with undisguised envy. Where British Colonialism saw a country of backwards heathens who worshipped at the altars of strange gods, Blavatsky saw a culture that was hundreds of years older than anything that could be boasted about in the West. Furthermore, she saw a culture that possessed a rare and profound knowledge of the metaphysical practices that she and her society sought to better understand.

Blavatsky's sympathy for India helped give the Theosophical Society new direction. Under her guiding hand, their new goals included the establishment of an idealized Universal Brotherhood that would be blind to color, race, or creed, the study of India's metaphysical tradition and scripture, and an overall investigation of all the spiritual and psychic mysteries of nature. Although some might find Blavatsky's appropriation of Hindu mysticism and beliefs less than flattering, her work nevertheless inspired appreciation for Indian culture in her largely British and American audience. She was so successful in creating Indian sympathizers that for at least a little while she was suspected of being a spy who worked in direct opposition of British Colonial efforts.

The Theosophical Society was indelibly stamped with Blavatsky's passions and beliefs, and, after her death in 1891, the society stumbled a little in her absence. Significant figures who rose to the top included Annie Besant and Rudolph Steiner. Steiner eventually moved on to found Anthroposophy. Besant could easily be credited with shaping the beliefs of the New Age.

Post-Blavatsky, there were several schisms along the way, but the society never died out entirely. The Theosophical Society remains active today, both in America and on an international level, and the influence of Theosophical beliefs can still be seen throughout much of the modern mystical movement.

Wide World of Weird

Dream Prediction?

WITNESS TO MURDER

What would it be like to witness a loved one's murder in a dream and be completely unable to prevent the tragedy? This was the horror facing one George Northey as recounted by psychical researcher William T. Stead.

George Northey worked as a sailor, but prior to that, he had lived with his brother Hart and their father. The two brothers were so close that they were never known to be apart. As they grew older and had to support themselves, George took to the ocean while Hart joined their father in the family's mercantile business.

In February, 1840, as George slumbered uneasily in his berth, he experienced an incredibly vivid dream. In this dream, he was back with his brother Hart Northey at Trebodwina Market. George followed Hart closely as the other man made transactions and picked up a large sum of coin from the family's trade. As the dream wore on, George became increasingly convinced that he was not bodily present with Hart but was rather like a projected spirit. While he could see and hear all that transpired around his brother, George could neither make himself seen nor heard.

This became an urgent problem as George began to sense that something very bad awaited Hart within the dream. As Hart finished his affairs at Trebodwina Market, he mounted his horse and took off down the road. George's point of perception continued to follow him, but his brother was still utterly insensible to his presence. A growing anxiety caused George to try again and again to make himself known to his brother. He wanted to warn him, particularly once Hart began to approach the hamlet of Polkerrow. As Hart rode along the dusty path between stands of trees, George was overcome with a "perfect frenzy" and he frantically strove to communicate to his sibling.

But he could not, and he was helpless to watch as two men appeared from either side of the road. George recognized them as the Hightwood brothers, a pair of notorious poachers who lived in the woods near St. Eglos.

Hart knew the men as well, and he paused in his ride as they asked about some work that had been promised to them. The civilities did not last long, however, and the men soon demanded Hart's coin. When he refused to give it, he was shot. George, still mute and invisible, was forced to watch his brother's lifeless body pitch from the saddle and tumble to the road.

But the dream wasn't over. George remained to watch as one of the ruffians strangled Hart, just to be sure the man was dead. Then they stripped the corpse of any valuables and dragged it to a nearby ditch. They covered all traces of blood on the roadway and sent the horse to gallop away. Finally, they took the pistol and hid it in the thatch roof of a nearby abandoned cottage.

When George awoke, he was certain the dream had been real and his brother Hart was dead. But he had a day's journey ahead before he could confirm his awful suspicion. Once his ship arrived home, he received the news: Hart was dead, murdered on the road to Polkerrow. The two poachers were prime suspects, but no one could find the pistol with which Hart had been shot. It was then that George intervened, telling the authorities where to search in the thatching of the little cottage.

The pistol was hidden exactly as he had seen it in the dream. The Hightwood brothers confessed and were executed. Although George had been powerless to prevent Hart's murder, at least his nightly visitation helped guarantee justice for the dead.

> *Out of body experience, witnessing a murder.*

The Magi of the Drawing Room

During the days of Jack the Ripper, occultism was all the rage in London. The British empire had already been introduced to a variety of unusual beliefs, both through the advent of Spiritualism as well as the influence of Helena Petrovna Blavatsky's organization, the Theosophical Society. And then a London coroner, Dr. William Westcott, decided to get together with his rather colorful friend, S. L. Macgregor Mathers to found what is known to the world as the Hermetic Order of the Golden Dawn. Together with Dr. W. R. Woodman, Supreme Magus of the Rosicrucian Society of Anglia, they formed the three chiefs of the Order.

Westcott, who was a Mason, claimed to have access to a mysterious cipher, connected to a German Rosicrucian, Anna Sprengel. Mathers took the material in the cipher and developed an elaborate ritual system from the information it contained. Drawing heavily upon traditional ceremonial magic, ancient Egyptian mysticism, and the Jewish Kabbalah, the ritual system of the Golden Dawn remains highly influential even today.

Between 1888 and 1896, over three hundred initiations were performed. The Order attracted a wide variety of members, drawing primarily from the London literati of the day. Members included the poet W. B. Yeats, Constance Wilde (wife of the far more famous Oscar Wilde), actresses Anni Horniman and Florence Farr, and learned occultists Israel Regardie and A. E. Waite. Aleister Crowley, who would later found his own magickal societies and scandalize the world by styling himself the Great Beast, was also first involved in the Golden Dawn (Crowley is such a larger-than-life figure that he's been the inspiration for a series of devilish creations, from an Ozzy Osbourne song to a long-standing character on *Supernatural*).

If you have ever read the Tarot, you have likely been exposed to some of the Golden Dawn's lingering influence. The most standard template for modern Tarot decks is based upon the Rider-Waite deck, named in part for occultist A.E. Waite, who developed the deck. Pamela Colman-Smith, known as Pixie to her friends, was responsible for the striking and mystic artwork – although her name is frequently (and unfairly) left out of the title of the deck.

In-fighting caused strife within the Order by the turn of the Twentieth Century. Issues were particularly heated between Mathers and Crowley, who allegedly engaged in a series of vicious psychic attacks upon one another. Ultimately, the organization shattered into splinter groups, some of which lingered on through the 1940s. There are several groups around today that still claim a direct lineage to the original Golden Dawn, including the Horus Temple and the Esoteric Order of the Golden Dawn.

THE LADY FROM HEAVEN

The sky was clear near *Cova da Iria* on the afternoon of May 13, 1917. The Portuguese countryside was idyllic. Then there was a flash in the sky and a figure appeared. The figure was a woman robed in white and, in the words of one witness, she was "radiating a light more clear and intense than a crystal cup filled with sparkling water, lit by burning sunlight." Over the next six months, the figure would appear, often just after the sky flashed as if with lightning. She would depart by rising into the sky. That was where she was from, after all.

The lady, witnessed first by three children ranging between the ages of seven and ten, was identified as none other than the Virgin Mary. The apparitions, which took place on the thirteenth day of the month from May to October, were eventually witnessed by thousands. Beyond the rural village of Fatima in Portugal, Europe was torn asunder by the violence and bloodshed of the First World War. And according to the children, the Virgin had appeared to help the world repair its ways and seek peace.

When the Lady of Fatima first appeared to young Lucia dos Santos and her two younger cousins, Francisco and Jacinta Marto, they already knew that she must be from Heaven. In the spring of the previous year, an angel had appeared to them three times. Like the benevolent Lady, he, too, had been clothed in shining robes and he possessed a dazzling beauty that words could not easily express.

Given the youth of the first three witnesses, villagers and local authorities were skeptical of their claims. When the appearances of the Virgin at Fatima had gained national attention, secular newspapers like *O Seculo* wrote satirically of the visions, strongly criticizing the whole phenomenon.

Reporter Avelino de Almedia, one of the authors of the critical articles that had appeared in *O Seculo* would later change his tune. Along with thousands of others, he had traveled to the site of the appearances on the date of the final appearance, October 13, 1917. The day was beset by a terrible storm, and by the time that the crowd had gathered near the old holmoak tree where the Virgin typically appeared, everyone was bedraggled and soaked. The children were undaunted and prayed for their Lady to appear. The appearance of the Lady before so many witnesses was not the greatest miracle of that day. Mary had promised to show the spectators something amazing that would earn their faith, and, from the accounts of hundreds of people, she delivered on that promise.

The event is known as the Miracle of the Sun. According to witnesses, the leaden clouds suddenly parted, and the sun seemed to appear like a dull gray disc in the sky. This disc began the shift and dance, throwing colors and whirling like a Catherine's wheel. The crowd panicked as the very sun seemed to descend from the heavens, and its heat dried their wet and muddy clothes in the space of ten minutes. When this whirling disc of colored light that witnesses identified with the sun was finished with its display, it returned to the heavens, as did the Lady of Fatima herself. Witnesses at a distance from the crowd of faithful saw something in the sky as the clouds parted, and their testimonies have been used to argue against the notion of mass delusion.

Only a very few researchers have dared to suggest the other alternative explanation to the Fatima appearances:

alien contact. In a flash of light, a figure appears, and she herself glows with unearthly light. She bathes the children in rays of light from her hands, and they are overcome with feelings of peace. And the mysterious disc in the sky, so immense that it could only be mistaken for the sun is unaccountably the dull gray of metal, bright, but certainly not brilliant like the sun. It further behaves in a manner very unlike any true heavenly body -- but a flying saucer could certainly dip down close enough to the crowd to dry them with its radiant heat.

Were the appearances at Fatima truly miraculous visions of the Virgin? Or could the appearances be explained through contact with an advanced race, a race that understood enough of our human limitations to allow spectators to interpret such advanced beings as connected with God?

Whatever the true nature of the visions, many of the prophecies handed down at Fatima later came true. Some were considered so earth-shattering that they were only revealed to the public as recently as 2000. True to the Virgin's word, the siblings Jacinta and Francisco died young, only after much suffering. Lucia lived to a ripe old age, keeping the secret prophecies and devoting her life to the service of the being who had singled her out for such revelations in her youth.

Wide World of Weird

KANSAS CITY VAMPIRE CULT

Did a cult of blood-drinkers terrorize Kansas City in the 1890s? The *Brooklyn Eagle* -- the paper Walt Whitman used to work for – certainly seemed to think so. An article ran on January 27th, 1890, warning people about a so-called "vampire cult." Notably, this was a full seven years before Bram Stoker's novel *Dracula* would make vampires a common house-hold word.

The Kansas City vampire cult was a significant problem, as another story about the group appeared about a week later in the *Dallas Weekly Times Herald*. Here it was published under the more colorful headline: "Nest of Bloodsuckers. The Horrible Orgies of a New Sect at Kansas City." Curiously, this article reveals that the bloodsuckers were a new sect of Christians who had adopted some fairly unusual healing practices based on the line from Leviticus that states, "the blood is the life." Read on:

Nest of Bloodsuckers
The Horrible Orgies of a New Sect at Kansas City
February 1, 1890

For some time, rumors of the existence of a new religious sect, which has gained a foothold in the territory adjacent to the Blue river, just east of Kansas City, have been afloat and they have reached the ears of the police. The secretary of the Humane Society recently received a letter from a man living in that neighborhood telling him that if the authorities did not interfere the people would take the matter in their own hands.

According to the reports the practices of the sect were founded upon the Biblical injunction "to do good to the sick," but this injunction had been carried to such an extent that the sect had degenerated into a band of blood suckers. Those who were well allowed themselves to be bled for those who were ill.

Officer Moran's investigation of the matter proved that the letter to Secretary Huckett had not told half of the horrible practices in vogue among the people who believe in the savage rites. About a year ago there appeared among the people of that neighborhood a man named Silas Wilcox, who went about the country preaching the doctrine of doing good for the sick. It was not long until he had a sufficient number of converts to his theories to warrant him in founding a sect, which he called the *Samaritans*. Gradually he widened his teachings to his little band until he openly advocated the drinking of blood for all diseases, giving as authority for such action the fact that the Bible taught that the blood was life.

At the home of John Wrinkle were found two emaciated children. On the bed lay Wrinkle's wife, who was apparently in the last stages of consumption. When questioned about drinking the blood of the children he strenuously denied having done so. The children also denied it. Their bloodless appearance, however, excited the suspicion of the officers and he compelled them to show their arms. Their limbs were in a terrible condition, being covered with scars around the inside of the elbow joints, showing plainly the effects of the bleeding. When confronted with this evidence of the truth of the accusation Wrinkle acknowledged that he had availed himself of the opportunity and asserted that the children had willingly given their blood to restore him to health. The man was in such a condition that he could not be moved, but the children were taken from the house and placed in the Children's Home.

Chief Spears is anxious to put a stop to the practice of blood drinkers but it appears there is no law which covers the case and nothing can be done.

Notably, online records survive showing a Wrinkle family living in the Kansas City area at the time of the story. Their patriarch was named "John H." However, there's no clear record indicating that he had two sons.

Did John and his wife extend their lives by sucking the blood of their children? It sounds preposterous, and yet modern experiments have been conducted that claim to help aging rats by injecting them with the blood of the young.

THE BLOOD COUNTESS

Elizabeth Bathory (Báthory Erzsébet, in her native Hungarian) was a beautiful woman of noble birth who came into this world on August 7, 1560. History remembers her as the "Blood Countess." Between the years of 1585 and 1610, she allegedly tortured over six hundred girls and young women, killing them all. If these numbers hold true, she remains one of the most prolific serial killers of all time.

Elizabeth was married young to Count Ferencz Nadasdy, a man ten years her senior. After their marriage, they moved to a castle overlooking the town of Csejthe in north-western Hungary. Ferencz was a soldier first, and a husband second, and so young Elizabeth was often left at home to while away her days as her husband fought on the battlefield. He would later become known as the "Black Hero of Hungary," but poor Elizabeth was overwhelmed with boredom.

It seems that she chose some strange occupations to fill her time. She was already known to be promiscuous: married at 15, she did not go to her marriage bed a virgin. Prior to her marriage, she'd had a child out of wedlock by a peasant man. At the castle, with her husband so often away, she took a number of young men to her bed in succession, and she even tried to run off with one of them. She returned and was given her husband's forgiveness. Perhaps he was willing to turn a blind eye to sexual indiscretions so long as no illegitimate children resulted from her unions, for Elizabeth seems to have turned to homosexual liaisons thereafter. She paid frequent visits to her aunt, the Countess Klara Bathory, who was openly bisexual. She also spent a great deal of time with a maid, Anna Darvula. Anna was alleged to be Elizabeth's lover and one of the people who encouraged her sadistic affairs.

At first, Elizabeth only preyed upon females of the lower classes. Peasants and servant girls were rarely missed, and even if their parents knew what had become of their beloved children, there was little they could do to bring accusations against a noble of Bathory's standing. But eventually, Bathory's depravity depopulated the local villages of likely victims. In a clever gambit to get more girls sent her way, Bathory started what amounted to a finishing school, encouraging lesser nobles to send their daughters to her castle to be trained in etiquette and other courtly affairs. When these daughters also began disappearing, finally an investigation was launched, and Bathory's many crimes began to come to light.

Bathory's own cousin, György Thurzó, working as the Palatine of Hungary (second only to the king), raided her castle on December 29, 1610. The sights he witnessed there horrified him and his men.

Elizabeth's accomplices were brought almost immediately to trial. Most of the accomplices were servants who worked in Elizabeth's household, including an old maid named Dorottya Szentes, who was allegedly a practicing witch. The Royal Supreme Court of Hungary convened on January 7, 1611 to begin hearing testimonies. Among the accusations levied against Elizabeth and her accomplices were that she starved the girls in her keeping, sometimes allowed them to freeze to death, would burn or mutilate their hands and sometimes also their faces and genitals, and that she would beat the girls for extended periods of time, often bludgeoning them literally to death.

In keeping with the vampire theme which Bathory's blood lust seems to have earned, she was also accused of often biting her victims, chewing gobbets of flesh from their faces, arms, and other body parts – while they were still alive.

The January trials led to the deaths of all of Elizabeth's accomplices. Elizabeth herself, as a woman of noble birth, could not suffer the same fate as her lessors. Instead, she was walled up in a single room of her castle and made to live out the rest of her days, deprived completely of human company. She was found face-down in this makeshift cell only four years later, quite dead.

Even though such allegations never came out in the trial, most modern accounts of Elizabeth Bathory assert that she bathed in the blood of her victims. This detail, along with the fact that she was distantly related to Prince Vladimir III of Wallachia, known to the world as Dracula, has established Elizabeth firmly in the annals of the vampire myth. But where did the notion that she bathed in blood come from, if not from her own depraved practices?

In 1729, during a time when scientific and governing authorities throughout Eastern Europe were concerned with outbreaks of vampirism, the Jesuit scholar László Turócziproduced the first written account of Bathory's life and crimes. In his book, he alleged that Bathory bathed in the blood of her victims, presumably to retain her youth and beauty. Although this motive for her crimes remains the most memorable one, it begins in Turóczi's book and does not appear in any of the actual court records concerning her crimes. Nevertheless, Turóczi's writing very firmly connected Bathory's name with the growing vampire craze of his times, and the late Raymond T. McNally argued that author Bram Stoker seized upon

Bathory's legend as part of the inspiration for his own vampire tale. Due to the nature of myth and legend, regardless of her actual practices, Bathory's blood-thirsty acts have guaranteed her continued association with vampires in the popular imagination.

THE GHOST'S AFOOT!

Sir Arthur Conan Doyle (1859-1930) is the Scottish author best known for his sleuthing literary creation, Sherlock Holmes. Doyle's fictional detective epitomizes the powers of deductive reasoning and rational thought, so it may come as a surprise to some Holmes fans that Doyle himself harbored a life-long fascination for the paranormal. Doyle developed a taste for the tales of Edgar Allan Poe early in life, but his interest in spirits and paranormal phenomenon can be traced back to a specific experience in 1887.

Doyle, who worked as a surgeon in addition to penning mystery tales, was visiting a patient's house when the other residents were sitting for a séance. Intrigued, Doyle joined in the fun. At the time, Spiritualism was all the rage, and table-tipping was a fairly common parlor past-time.

For a little while, nothing happened, and the sitters merely engaged in a lively conversation. And then, as Doyle himself records in his notebooks, the table began to move with a jerking motion, using Morse code to tap out messages from the spirits. For Doyle, the experience rendered the uncertainty of religion moot. He felt that spirit communication proved the existence of an afterlife beyond the shadow of a doubt, and he viewed Spiritualism as something akin to a science of the Otherside.

From that point forward, Doyle was hooked on ghosts, although he did not "come out" as a Spiritualist until after the First World War. His literary creation, the ever-astute Holmes, was, by contrast, critical of the paranormal. In "The Adventure of the Sussex Vampire,"

Doyle even has Holmes jokingly state, "This agency stands flat-footed upon the ground, and there it must remain. The world is big enough for us. No ghosts need apply."

Some of Doyle's hesitancy for coming out may have been related to concerns for his political connections. Doyle was one of several famous authors from his time (including H.G. Wells, G.K. Chesterton, and Rudyard Kipling) who sat in on a secret meeting of the War Propaganda Bureau in 1914. The goal of the conference was to discuss the best methods of promoting Britain's interests during the war. Subsequent to the meeting, Doyle wrote several pamphlets for the war effort, including the recruiting pamphlet *To Arms!* and "A Visit to the Three Fronts."

After World War I, Doyle became much more open about his beliefs, penning a number of books on spiritualism, including *The New Revelation* and *The History of Spiritualism*. Doyle also became embroiled with friend Harry Houdini's attempt to discredit mediums, and their clash of opinions ultimately severed their friendship. Near the end of his life, Doyle gained a reputation for being somewhat overly credulous of the paranormal. This was largely due to his unflagging support of the Cottington Fairy Photographs, images reportedly taken by two Yorkshire girls, starting in 1917 (which has since been definitively proven a hoax).

M. Belanger

EDISON'S QUEST TO TALK TO THE DEAD

Inventor Thomas Edison (1847-1931) is typically portrayed as the archetypal "modern man of science," a figure as immersed in the revolutionary beliefs of the scientific age as he was immersed in the vision of his genius. As the holder of one thousand and ninety-three patents, one might be tempted to believe that Edison was a hard-nosed man of science, utterly dedicated to the cold, hard truths of technology. And yet the "Wizard of Menlo Park" not only had a passion for science and electricity. He also expressed a marked fascination with the realm of the paranormal.

Significantly influenced by the Spiritualist movement, which had started in the 1800s, but enjoyed a revival right after World War I, Edison believed in something he designated "life units." These "life units" were the indestructible constituent parts of the soul. When a man's body died and decayed, these particles simply rearranged themselves, and the intelligence of the man lived on. In Edison's schema, the so-called "Spirit world" was nothing more than the staging ground where all these indestructible units waited. It was all around us, but it existed outside of the reach of our gross physical perceptions -- but he felt that a machine could be produced that was finely tuned enough to pick up communications from the life units floating around us.

In October 1920, *American Magazine* ran an article declaring that Edison was working just such an invention -- a machine that would enable him to communicate with ghosts. For many modern paranormal investigators, this makes the father of the phonograph and the lightbulb also the father of the very concept of EVP (Electronic Voice Phenomenon).

In the same month, Austin Lescarbouras of the *Scientific American*, interviewed Edison on the topic of life after death. Edison is quoted as saying, "I don't claim that our personalities pass onto another existence ... But I do claim that it is possible to construct an apparatus which will be so delicate that if there are personalities in another existence who wish to get in touch with us... this apparatus will at least give them a better opportunity."

Allegedly, Edison labored in secret on the machine in the last years of his life. No one ever saw it, although the magician Joseph Dunniger, claimed to have been shown a prototype. Perhaps the Great Inventor of the 20th Century instinctively knew that he was racing against time in the construction of his apparatus. Perhaps he held out hope that his final invention would allow others to reach out to him across the void, enabling him to continue to enrich our lives with his genius. Whatever the case, Edison died before completing his fantastic spirit-communication machine. Although Edison's journals and papers talk of his work on the machine, the actual plans for the apparatus, highly sought after, were never found.

On an even eerier note, at the moment of Edison's death, it is reported that each and every clock in his house stopped at precisely the same time. Perhaps the spirits of the machines themselves were making an effort to mourn the passing of the man who had brought so many of their technological brethren to life.

But How Much for the Postage?

Ancient Egypt. Almost everything that the world has left of this ancient civilization is tied directly to their tombs. Of all the world's great civilizations, the ancient Egyptians had, perhaps, the most well-developed funerary tradition, and their beliefs in the afterlife were tied to beliefs in a complex species of soul.

In the cosmology of ancient Egypt, each individual was thought to possess not one, but several spirits. Among these was the Akh, the immortal spirit, typically represented by a glyph that resembled the Benu bird -- the inspiration for the Greek Phoenix, itself a potent symbol of immortality and rebirth.

There was the Ba, a winged spirit with the body of a bird and the head of a man, which flew forth from the corpse upon death. And then there was the Ka, whose hieroglyph was two upraised arms. The image of the Ka, depicted on the left, is shown wearing its hieroglyph like a crown. In modern occult writings, the Ka is often equated with the metaphysical notion of the Body Double, the portion of the self fundamental to astral projection. This spirit was the perfect twin of the deceased, and it was believed to remain lingering in the tomb, tied to the mortal remains so carefully mummified by Egyptian morticians.

According to displays at the Kelsey Museum in Ann Arbor, MI, the Ka "required sustenance in the afterlife, and relatives or priests would make offerings in front of the false door." The false door was a structure that allowed the tomb to remain sealed, but symbolically permitted the Ka to leave the tomb, should it so choose.

Of course, your average ancient Egyptian didn't like to be followed around by dead relatives any more than the next guy, and so the offerings were made to keep the Ka fat and happy in the tomb. This had the added benefit of discouraging this earth-bound ghost from wandering around the countryside, seeking sustenance from other sources.

Despite these precautions, the ancient Egyptian dead did not always stay put. There are numerous letters that have come down to us from this ancient culture, written by the living and addressed to the dead. It seems that, when signs of a haunting began to occur, it was customary to address the dead person and politely request that they leave the living alone. In addition to nicely asking the dead to stop haunting them, the beleaguered family member would also promise to make bigger and better offerings to make it worth the spirit's while to hang out in their tomb.

DANCING WITH DEATH

What would you do if you met Death? Artist Leilah Wendell would embrace him like an old friend. She claims to have met the personification of Death – both spiritually and physically – and through her art and her writing, she professes her devotion to this often-misunderstood entity.

Wendell is the founder of the Azrael Project, an organization devoted to the study of the personification of Death in the figure of the angel Azrael. In the 90s, the Azrael Project involved a physical newsletter in addition to the House of Death, a combination art gallery and museum devoted to Azrael, located in New Orleans. As the times and technology have changed, Wendell moved her tribute to Death onto the Internet as well.

Wendell has had experiences with Azrael since childhood, and she has made it her life's work to chronicle her relationship with this entity. She tells his story in her underground classic, *Our Name is Melancholy,* and she founded The Azrael Project to seek out stories from others who feel that their lives have been touched by this solemn and sometimes forbidding being.

Wendell, a talented artist who also runs the Westgate Gallery, does not see Death as evil or even frightening. From her paintings, it is clear that she finds Azrael to be a romantic figure. Her writings typify him as a gentle being who comes to release us of our burdens, and whose gifts include the cessation of pain. Some may find Wendell's fascination unsettling, and a few have accused her of bordering upon necrophilia in her portrayals of Azrael, but since the 90s, her work has attracted a core of very devoted fans. She herself has been unflagging in her dedication to Azrael, and she has collected a massive amount of material documenting individual sightings of what certainly seems to be the very personification of Death.

THE HAUNTING OF JACKSON SQUARE

New Orleans is an incredibly haunted city. In the French Quarter alone, it seems as if you cannot turn the corner without encountering a ghost. While there are many tales that can be told of the restless spirits tied to this delta city, few are more poignant than the ghostly requiem alleged to play on rainy nights in Jackson Square.

During the Spanish occupation of New Orleans, French loyalists staged an uprising the thwart the foreign crown. After a bloody struggle, the uprising was brutally put down. Most of the rebels were killed, and their bodies were stored in the church at Jackson Square. Despite the protests of the local priest, the bodies of the insurrectionists were denied burial by the Spanish authorities.

Late one night, in a torrential Louisiana downpour, the local citizens stole into the church, wrapped the bodies, and carried them off to hallowed ground. As the rain poured down upon them, the mourners solemnly lifted their voices in a traditional Requiem.

Jackson Square is well-known to be haunted. The haunting, however does not involve the spirits of the men who were killed. Instead, each time the rain pours from the skies over the city, the ethereal notes of the mourners can be heard just over the roar of the rain.

DOES MY INSURANCE COVER IT?

Psychic surgery is a popular method of alternative medicine practiced widely in Indonesia. Although they are not medically trained, psychic surgeons claim to be able to remove tumors and even kidney stones from the body with the power of their minds. Psychic surgeons do not cut into their patients, but despite this, blood flows and strange-looking gobbets of flesh are pulled from the sick person as family members watch. James Randi feels confident that he has proven this practice a hoax, claiming that psychic surgeons use sleight of hand to palm packets of blood and chicken giblets before the surgery so that spectators will have a bloody show to prove that something is being removed.

Although the reality of this method of psychic surgery is a matter of debate, there are a number of other techniques that seem to harness the power of the mind for healing. Reiki, Qi-Gong, and Barbara Ann Brennan's technique, *Hands of Light*, are all variations on the old method of "laying on of hands," using human touch and energy to heal illness and disease. Although these techniques are also somewhat controversial, energy healing has been implemented by some Western hospitals as a supplemental therapy for terminal cancer, and a number of nurses have added a Reiki degree to their repertoire of certified therapies because they feel the energetic healing techniques can complement more traditional Western medical approaches.

Does it work? Experiments performed at the prestigious Cleveland Clinic seem to suggest that it does. In an experiment involving individuals undergoing physical therapy, one group was taught to do energy work while also performing their regular physical therapy routine. The other group has given physical therapy with no energy work whatsoever. Although the results of the energy work were not miraculous by any stretch, they did provide enough of a statistical difference in the participants' results to indicate that a combined approach can help people heal better and over a shorter period of time.

Capturing the Light of Life?

Kirlian photography is a method of high voltage imaging developed by a Russian husband and wife team. Semyon Davidovich Kirlian and his wife Valentina began their work with high voltage photography starting in 1939. For the next thirty years, they researched their technique, and in 1970, their research came to the attention of American audiences through Shelia Ostrander's classic, *Psychic Discoveries Behind the Iron Curtain*.

Kirlian photography claims to record images of the energy field of living things. Often presented as a method of aura photography, what Kirlian photography is really capturing is the electro-magnetic field natural to humans, animals, and plants. The method for constructing a Kirlian camera is deceptively simple. A lightless chamber is prepared, and, at the bottom, there is a metal plate, set up to receive a mild electrical charge. The unexposed film is placed directly onto this plate, and the item to be photographed -- often a leaf or flower -- is placed on top of the film. Then an electrical pulse is sent through the plate. This exposes the film, which records an image of the object, typically outlined with what appears to be colored light. When human fingertips or hands are placed in camera upon the film, the resulting image shows a nimbus of light extending out around the skin. This is the radiant energy of the human body, amplified by the electrical charge and captured on the film.

Of course, as with every method that claims to record some aspect of the paranormal, Kirlian photography has been decried by skeptics as nothing but camera trickery. The most balanced argument skeptics have come up with is that the resulting aura captured on the film is really nothing more than a cloud of ionization produced through the combination of the electrical charge and the natural moisture around the hand or other object being photographed.

This author has had the opportunity to indulge in experiments using a small Kirlian Lab camera, set up to take images using the Kirlian method. While it was clear that the electrical charge was pivotal to the exposure of any image on the film, it also became clear after multiple images that each person whose fingertips were photographed by the camera had a unique and recognizable pattern – an energetic fingerprint, as it were. Even changing the length and strength of the electrical pulse that exposed the film, this specific pattern remained true. Changing the charge only changed how brightly it showed up on the film. This consistency argues that the Kirlian method is indeed photographing something more than just ambient electricity conducted through the object or person through the metal plate.

But does the Kirlian method accurately record an image of the human aura, with colors and patterns that can be interpreted with specific meanings? That aspect of this fascinating method remains to be seen.

THE FATHER OF GHOST-HUNTING

When it comes to modern research into ghost-hunting, few figures have been more prolific than Austrian-born Hans Holzer. The author of over one hundred and thirty books, he has an impressive body of work, and that's not counting his many television scripts, plays, and musicals (he learned conducting at Julliard!). All of his writings involve some aspect of the occult, and his non-fiction has provided several foundational books on ghosts, hauntings, and witchcraft, including *Ghost Hunter,* published in 1963, and *Wicca: The Way of the Witches*, published in 1979.

Through his book, *Ghost Hunter,* Holzer is often credited with coining the term. This is not entirely accurate, as Harry Price was using the word back in the 1930s. However, Holzer is certainly one of the main forces responsible for popularizing the idea of ghost-hunting, particularly through his very visible work with the Amityville Horror case.

In addition to hunting ghosts and working with mediums, Holzer has a background in comparative religions. In the 1960s, this led him to investigate the growing tradition of witchcraft in the United Kingdom. There, he interviewed many of the modern witches practicing in that country, helping the rest of the world achieve a better understanding of this mystical nature religion. He was even initiated into the craft himself. During this time, Holzer also found an intersection between his inquiries into witchcraft and his ghost-hunting. This was facilitated through the person of Sybil Leek who, in addition to her identity as a witch was also a skilled spirit-medium. In this, Holzer was ahead of the curve is recognizing that the practices of modern witches are not limited only to magick but also include a variety of psychic abilities and spirit-work as well.

Holzer is a world-traveler and has investigated hauntings all over the globe. He lectures on occult topics at a variety of colleges and conventions and, for a time, taught parapsychology at the New York Institute of Technology. When he is not traveling, Holzer resides in Manhattan's Upper West Side, where he maintains a massive private collection of paranormal and occult curios.

RETOOLING PARANORMAL TECHNOLOGY

Very few tools of the ghost-hunter's trade were made expressly for sensing the presence of spirits. As with gauss meters and thermographic cameras, the vast majority of gadgets that are currently used in the paranormal field were developed for much more mundane work. One of the biggest reasons for this is the experimental nature of paranormal work, and the fact that, although most ghost-hunters agree that spirits are comprised of energy, no one has yet hit upon a specific frequency where they show up the best.

This situation presents an amazing opportunity for the inventive ghost-hunter. New technology is being produced every year by individuals with backgrounds in electronics or other sciences. But why break with tradition by completely reinventing the wheel? There are a vast number of ready-made sensing devices that, like the standard EMF reader, are already being used to pick up fluctuations in heat, light, pressure, and other atmospheric variables. It simply remains for someone to apply their use to the field of paranormal research in order to see if spirits and other phenomenon can influence these fine-tuned instruments as well.

One example of possible para-tech is the scintillometer. Have you ever seen the shimmer of heat on a distant patch of road on a hot summer's day? This device reads that shimmer, called a scintillation. The effect is caused by variations in temperature, humidity, and pressure between the surface of the earth and the air directly above it. The device also enables scientists to measure something known as "sensible heat" -- the transfer of heat that occurs between the atmosphere and the earth's surface. This is not an indoor device -- the scintillometer measures atmospheric fluctuations over miles -- but the data it collects may nevertheless have paranormal applications.'

Given the influence that spirits have been known to have upon ambient temperature, most notably in the form of cold spots, could this device have an application within the paranormal field? What sort of anomalous readings might a scintillometer be capable of picking up if its target area included a haunted battlefield or even the reported landing site of a UFO? Only those willing to explore the very cutting edge of paranormal technology – and freely pillage tech from other disciplines – may ever know.

POE'S GRIM PROPHECY

Edgar Allan Poe, who lived between 1809 and 1849, was an American poet, writer, and literary critic best known for the supernatural and macabre themes twining throughout his work. As brilliant as he was melancholy, many of Poe's short stories contained bitter commentary on the human condition – particularly observations on how far humans could be driven by grief, greed, vengeance, or desperation.

One classic example of the latter is the 1838 Poe short story entitled, "The Narrative of Arthur Gordon Pym of Nantucket." The tale revolves around a shipwreck, focusing on the four miserable survivors who are left adrift at sea. Starving, desperate, and dying of thirst with no rescue in sight, the men come to a terrible decision: they will draw lots among them and whoever loses will be killed and eaten so the others may survive. The lot falls to Richard Parker, and he is summarily sacrificed and consumed.

This is a grisly tale, to be sure, but why mention it on a blog devoted to the paranormal? Unlike so many of Poe's short stories, "The Narrative of Arthur Gordon Pym of Nantucket" contains no obvious supernatural elements.

That is, until nearly fifty years later, when it proved to be prophetic.

In 1884, four men survived a shipwreck. They lingered, adrift, for many days until they were nearly overcome with thirst, hunger, and the elements. The first to weaken among them was the ship's cabin boy. Overcome with desperation, the other three murdered the cabin boy and ate him. Thus, they survived, although they were later tried for their act of murderous cannibalism.

The name of the cabin boy who met such a gruesome fate? Richard Parker, of course.

Is Hi Tech the Best Tech?

During a talk he gave at Univ-Con 2006, ghost-hunter Grant Wilson brought up an intriguing point. When seeking EVP and videographic evidence of ghosts, most people assume that high-tech devices are better than their lower-tech equivalents. Hi-end digital voice recorders have a greater sound acuity, but this might not work in a ghost-hunter's favor. That clearer sound arises from the device's ability to filter out non-essential signal. Essentially, as Grant suggested, the pricier, new-fangled equipment might just filter out the frequencies that carry signals such as EVP.

How many EVPs represent a sound that was not heard with human ears at the time of the recording? How many anomalies captured on video were invisible to the naked human eye? Many ghost-hunters use their equipment specifically because, psychics aside, the average person cannot reliably perceive the phenomenon. Most ghostly activity seems to occur somewhere beyond the range of humanity's five physical senses, and it stands to reason that if we continue to fine-tune our recording devices to more and more reliably zero in on just the frequencies perceptible by those five senses, we will inadvertently filter out the frequencies that carry the very phenomenon that ghost-hunters seek.

Ten or fifteen years ago, most folks chasing after the perfect EVP were limited to a cassette recorder. Anyone seeking orbs or a ghostly miasma floating across the screen had to rely upon some clunky, barely portable VHS camera in their attempt to capture it. Since then, technology has clipped along at a break-neck pace, giving us digital voice recorders, digital cameras, webcams, cell phones that have both cameras and voice recorders, and a host of new and generally expensive gadgets to play around with.

Don't have a digital recorder on hand? Open up your laptop and download a copy of Audacity, a free recording program used my many amateur podcasters. This program turns any computer into a mini-recording studio. But is it better than the old-standby of a tape recorder and cassette? That may depend not only on the program as well as your laptop's capabilities, but also on the quality of your microphone. In fact, there are so many factors to take into consideration with modern equipment, it's a wonder we don't all throw our hands in the air and go back to really low-tech methods, such as pendulums and Ouija boards.

The moral of this story is that bigger is not always better. It may not profit a ghost-hunter to stay on the cutting edge of modern technology, at least as far as audio and video recording devices are concerned. The best approach is to educate yourself thoroughly about your equipment, and know all of its quirks and capabilities. An intriguing approach, for those who can afford it, is to use both hi-tech and low-tech equipment and, at the end of the investigation, compare the results.

The Groovy Art of Stereomancy

In traditional divinatory techniques, "stereomancy" is the practice of divining through the elements. In this age of technology, however, the word has come to develop another meaning entirely: divination through the songs that play on your radio, iPod, or computer. It's hardly an official method of divination, but how many of us have experienced this phenomenon? You start your morning commute, and as you thread your way through the traffic, certain songs start playing on the radio that eerily echo your thoughts or current mood. Or you have your iPod on shuffle, but the same song keeps coming up over and over again. Something in the lyrics seems to be a message geared specifically to you, and later in the day, that message seems to come true.

It's easy to read too much into the things that randomly occur around us (apophenia is a genuine psychological condition), but messages out of apparent random actions is what most divinatory techniques are all about.

Divination can be seen to function on one of two principles. Either, there is a greater force that governs events in the world, so that patterns emerge, even from apparent chaos. Fans of fractals and chaos theory can even skip the implication that this guiding force is explicitly divine – in modern chaos theory, the force that causes complex patterns to emerge from the chaotic input of numbers in a fractal is simply a mathematical value known as a "strange attractor."

The other possibility is perhaps even more earth-shattering in its implications. Can we, as humans, have an influence on the apparently random activity that occurs around us? One researcher, Masaru Emoto, seems to have proven that human emotions can affect the structure and appearance of water crystals. At the more obscure ends of modern scientific theories, there are notions that the very act of observation can influence the activity of the thing being observed. This is known simply as the observer effect, and it suggests a profound and mysterious relationship between observation and *apparently* random phenomenon.

A lot has been made of this by arm-chair quantum physicists, but one experiment, which is on-going, really stands out. It involves a black box known as a Random Event Generator. The box randomly generates two numbers, a one and a zero, rather like the heads or tails of a coin. According to the laws of chance, these two options should each come up fifty percent of the time in a random dispersion. But one scientist, a Professor Jahn, wanted to see if human thought could influence the random generation of the numbers. His experiments in the 1970s led to a number of these black boxes being installed in universities around the world where they tantalizingly seem to predict major world events.

Does the REG prove the underlying principles of divination? Scientists are still working on that one, but maybe you should pay a little more attention to that song playing on the radio right now.

THE MYSTERIOUS CAT

The cat has been an object of mystery to many cultures throughout the ages. The ancient Egyptians worshipped the animal, and hundreds, if not thousands, of cats were accorded the rites of mummification, a complicated funerary practice typically reserved only for the nobility. Cats were held in such high regard in this culture that a human could incur the death penalty for killing one of these four-legged citizens.

Ancient Egypt was not alone in revering the cat. In many African and South American cultures, big cats, such as the jaguar or the leopard, were viewed with a comingling of fear and awe, and they became mythologized as gods, demons, or agents of the spirit world.

In the Middle Ages, cats had become objects of terror for many, associated with the Devil and witchcraft. In the time of the witch trials, it was not uncommon for cats to fall under suspicion of nefarious practices. Many witches were accused of keeping familiars, demonic spirits that assumed the shape of common animals, typically cats, dogs, or toads. During a time when Europeans were singling out fellow villagers and torturing them by the thousands under suspicion of witchcraft, cats were believed not only to act as familiar spirits but also to work for Satan even without the influence of a presiding witch.

In the 13th century, Pope Gregory IX issued a Papal Bull declaring all black cats to be agents of the Devil. Subsequently, thousands of cats were rounded up and burned alive in an attempt to protect the world from the influence of Satan.

Perhaps ironically, the wide-spread slaughter and mistrust of cats during this time period may have left certain areas more vulnerable to the Black Plague, as rodent populations boomed in the absence of industrious felines.

Some of the original fears of witchcraft were inspired by a belief that certain antisocial members of a community were visiting sickness and disease upon their neighbors either out of jealousy or revenge. Killing cats that were suspected of witchcraft was an attempt to bring order and health back to troubled times. Given that rats and mice tended to carry the fleas that spread disease, this course of action had the exact opposite effect.

Mapping the Unknown

In 1513, a highly respected admiral within the Turkish navy compiled a map of the world. His name was Piri Reis, and the map, lost to the modern world until its rediscovery in 1929, also bears his name. The map inspired a great deal of controversy when it was first uncovered by modern historians and that controversy continues to this day.

Professor of history, Charles Hapgood made the Piri Reis map one of the focal points of his 1966 book, *Maps of the Ancient Sea Kings*. He took the existence of the Piri Reis map, as well as a few other anomalous maps, as proof of an ancient sea-faring civilization which he stopped just shy of naming as Atlantis. Erich von Daniken, who is credited with first developing the "ancient astronaut" theory, sees the map as proof of an extraterrestrial influence on the technology of earth. Author Graham Hancock takes a similar stance on the aged piece of gazelle skin that comprises the Piri Reis map. But what's so special about this document?

First of all, the map depicts the coastlines of both North and South America. The coastline of North America is imperfect, but there are recognizable elements. The map indicates mountains just inland on the western coast of South America, in the relative position of the Brazilian highlands. The coastline of South America continues unbroken to the bottom of the map, where it curves around in such a way as to suggest what may be the coastline of Antarctica. Certainly, historians of forbidden archaeology have insisted that this is the case.

Another argument among forbidden archaeologists, starting with the respectable Charles Hapgood, is that this map demonstrates geographic knowledge that was unavailable at the time that it was drawn. Admiral Piri Reis himself adds to this mystique by stating in his marginal notations that he compiled the details of the map through a comparison of other, more ancient maps found in the Imperial Library at Constantinople. Some of these were said to date back to the fourth century BCE or earlier. Could he have possibly gotten the details of North and South America from these ancient maps? Or were the details that appear on the map reasonably known in the admiral's day?

Remember that Christopher Columbus had set off to discover the New World in 1492, two decades before Piri Reis compiled his map. John Cabot traveled to Newfoundland in 1498, and the Spaniards had achieved some spotty sightings of the southeastern coast of the US by the time that the map was compiled (to make no mention of what the Vikings might have known prior to the classic European "Age of Exploration"). Would the Turks have had access to the Spanish maps in order to place the Americas across the Atlantic? It's a reasonable assertion, but forbidden archaeologists can't resist suggesting that the Piri Reis map was actually based off of more ancient maps of the New World than Columbus himself might have been privy to.

Steven Dutch, of the Natural and Applied Sciences of the University of Wisconsin, Green Bay, makes a solid case for the fact that Antarctica appears nowhere on the Piri Reis map. He also argues that the map is oriented with a center in Spain, which would make sense if the maps of the New World had come from that adventurous land. The real mystery of the Piri Reis map, as Dutch notes, is the fact that it is only one half of the original map. Torn in half and lost through the ages, what might the other portion of Piri Reis map reveal?

THE WEEPING WOMAN OF THE RIO GRANDE

Her name is La Llorona. She is said to be tall and thin, and her beautiful face is perfectly framed with flowing black hair. She wears a gown of spectral white and she paces near rivers and creeks, crying in the night. Her name, pronounced "LAH yoh ROH nah" is Spanish for the "Weeping Woman," and according to legend, she was once a mortal woman who, having drowned her own children, is now condemned to walk the night ceaselessly in search of them.

In the folktales that had spread up and down the Rio Grande, her name, before she became La Llorona, was Maria Gonzales, and her crime, ultimately, came about because of spousal betrayal and spurned love.

She is no benign or gentle spirit. Even in death, La Llorona is still a murderess, and she seeks out children who are unwise enough to wander out in the night. If she can find living replacements for her own dead progeny, she will ruthlessly drag them down to a watery grave, visiting upon them the same punishment that doomed her own flesh and blood.

La Llorona is a legend as old as the Spanish occupation of the Americas, but, rather than fading away in the mists of time, she has persisted over the long centuries. There are tales of La Llorona even still in Mexico and the American Southwest. These tales are told primarily among Spanish-speaking people, but La Llorona has universal appeal, and, over time, her legend has spread. There are many variations on her sad tale, and each region where she appears seems to have a specific place believed to be haunted by this restless ghost.

Perhaps her widespread appeal should not be surprising. The legend of the Weeping Woman appears in many cultures, and the legend of La Llorona, although Spanish in origin, bears many striking similarities to tales from other locales, including those from the British Isles.

In Great Britain, the specter is not precisely a ghost but instead has ties to the Faery Folk. Most readers are no doubt familiar with the word "banshee," often used generally to describe a class of beings, but originally the Banshee was a discreet entity. Her name was *"Bean Sidhe,"* meaning "Woman of the raths" – prehistoric burial mounds that were later connected to the Faery Folk who were believed to inhabit them. In one of the classic tales surrounding La Llorona, the tolling of church bells chases the dread ghost away from a little boy who is about to be her victim. Bells have a potent apotropaic effect in many cultures, and in the faery lore of the British Isles, they are notably believed to ward off faeries.

The Scottish version of the Bean Sidhe was a washer woman, and her name is typically translated "Washer at the Ford." Like La Llorona, her appearances were connected to rivers and natural lakes. In the stories about her, she would be seen washing bloody sheets over and over again. In one version of the tale, she is thought to have been a mortal woman who died in childbirth. She weeps for the babe whose life was lost in her failed attempt to bring it into the world, and it is her own blood, the blood of childbed, that she seeks to purge from the sheets. In later versions of the Bean Sidhe tale, she became a harbinger of death, tied to very specific Irish family lines, and her unearthly wail foretold the death of a family member. The blood she washed from sheets, clothes, and even armor was the blood of the doomed.

This is not to say that La Llorona and the Banshee are the same being, but rather that they stem from the same collective impulse: a primordial fear of tragedy as contagion and the ability of the spirits to reach beyond the grave in order to claim for themselves companions on the Otherside.

FALLING OFF THE EDGE OF TIME
The Specter of 2012

The Mayan people, who flourished between 200 CE and 900 CE, had an advanced calendrical system that calculated time in Short Counts and Long Counts. They looked at time as a series of cycles, and, according to their Long Count, our current age will end on the Winter Solstice in 2012. A lot has been made in recent years of the Mayan Calendar and this ominous date. There is a strong New Age current that looks upon this quickly advancing time as a promise of change. In their view of things, 2012 will be a great time of spiritual evolution when the collective vibration of humanity will ascend to something better, brighter, and more advanced. Some believers in this point of view go so far as to assert that our very DNA will undergo an evolutionary change as part of this planetary ascension.

According to another school of thought, however, 2012 is a dark date that could bring about world-wide upheaval and destruction. Much of this is based upon the belief in a mysterious Planet X, sometimes called planet Nibiru, that is supposedly orbiting our solar system on an oblique angle in a cycle that brings it catastrophically near to earth every 3600 years. The name for planet Nibiru, and the belief that is has ties with extra-terrestrial beings once worshipped as ancient gods owes much to the writings of Zecharia Sitchin, a fringe intellectual and proponent of the Ancient Astronaut theory, who further asserts that the gods and goddesses of ancient Sumer were extraterrestrials.

Will 2012 be an apocalypse or an apotheosis? Or will the date slip by unnoticed as the Mayan calendrical odometer simply rolls over and starts anew? Any student of history can see that we are living in volatile times, and with all the political, climatological, and economic upheaval gripping our world, it is tempting to believe that something big is just around the corner. What will 2012 bring us? Only time will tell.

WHAT HAS TWO EYES, NO MOUTH AND A MELON HEAD?

Bill Bartlett doesn't know either, but he can tell you that he saw it on a dark night in April thirty years ago. Driving home with friends, Bartlett, then seventeen, spied a strange creature by a tree. He was going around forty-five miles an hour, and so he only caught a glimpse of the thing as he drove along Farm Street in Dover, Massachusetts.

Bartlett's two friends, engaged in animated conversation, missed seeing the creature -- but when Bartlett stopped the car some distance away, proposing that they return to the spot to investigate, they weren't taking any chances. None of the boys returned to see what, if anything, Bill had actually seen.

Bartlett's sighting puzzles him to this day. In his statement about the sighting, Bartlett is quoted as saying, "It looked like a baby's body with long arms and legs. It had a big head about the same size as the body, it was sort of melon shaped. The color of it was ... the color of people in the Sunday comics."

Bartlett's sighting probably would have been passed off as just a teenage prank, if it were not for two more incidents with the creature later dubbed the "Dover Demon." About two hours after Bartlett's sighting, a second teenager was walking home after seeing his girlfriend. John Baxter, aged fifteen, saw a figure approaching that looked, from a distance, like a person with a deformed head.

And here's where the story gets even stranger: Baxter approached the figure with open curiosity as he knew a young man who lived in the area who did indeed have a deformed head as the result of a childhood illness. Thinking at first that the figure was this individual, Baxter called out to it, only to receive no answer. The encounter began to grow eerie for Baxter as he neared the being, only to discern that it was far too small to be his acquaintance. He described it as being the size of someone who was five or six.

Uncertain now, Baxter stopped his approach, and the creature also ceased its approach. They stood on the dark stretch of country road, apparently regarding one another warily. Then the creature took off. In his own report, Baxter said, "...as I took this step it just ran so fast into the woods on my left. It was just so fast, you know, one second it was there and another second it wasn't and I could hear it going through the woods, across a stream -- a little brook."

Baxter's sighting occurred within less than a mile of the intersection of Miller Hill Road and Farm Street. The picture drawn by Baxter to indicate what had seen was identical to Bartlett's in all significant details.

That was it for the night of April twenty-first. But that was not it for the Dover Demon. Around midnight the following night, Abbey Brabham had her own encounter. She had been out with her boyfriend, eighteen-year-old William Taintor, and now he was taking her back to her home in Sherborn.

Abbey, then fifteen, was the first to see it. She spied a tannish, goat-sized creature crouching on the left-hand side of the road at the edge of a bridge. Her description of the creature also matched Bartlett's and Baxter's. She said, "...the head was very big and it was a very weird head... It had bright green eyes and the eyes just glowed like, they were just looking exactly at me." Her boyfriend Taintor caught only a glimpse of the creature before it dashed off. Their sighting also occurred near Farm Street and the site of the Bartlett's original encounter.

The sightings occurred over a two-mile area. Plotted on a map, they actually lay in a straight line to one another. Loren Coleman, the cryptozoologist who first investigated the sightings, determined that the boys had not conferred prior to their encounters and in fact only discussed the creature the next week at school. There have been some issues on the topic of credibility, most notably the fact that all of the witnesses were in their teens. Although Bartlett has stuck to his description of his encounter, in later investigations, his story about when he saw Baxter's drawing changed at least twice. Despite these inconsistencies, the case drew national attention and these days, the creature – whatever it really was -- is often included among the ranks of canonical cryptids such as Bigfoot, Mothman, and the Loch Ness Monster.

There is an eerie postscript to the Dover Demon story. As it turns out, Farm Street is the second-oldest road in Dover, and it has had a reputation for strange occurrences since the seventeenth century. There were rumors that a mysterious treasure had been buried near the road, and one early resident of Dover claimed to have seen the Devil himself riding horseback near a large rock that was a recognized landmark near Farm Street. Dover historian, Frank Smith, records that this rock was given the name "Polka rock."

Although that moniker may cause visions of Weird Al Yankovic to leap to mind for some, cryptozoologist

Coleman has noted its similarity to "Pooka rock," a word connected with trickster spirits from Celtic faerie folklore. Coleman has also noted the similarity of the creature's appearance to that of the Mannegishi, the "little people" of the nearby Cree Indians. These reclusive cousins of humanity were believed to live near rocks and rapids, have long, thin arms and legs, and big heads, but no nose. As a point of interest for this theory, all of the Dover sightings occurred within the vicinity of water.

What really appeared to those teens on the shadowed streets of Dover in 1977? Despite logging twenty-five hours of exhaustive investigative research, neither Coleman nor any of the other cryptozoologists later called in on the case has a solid answer. Whatever it was, the creature has not been seen since -- unless you count its recent appearance on T-shirts to mark the thirtieth anniversary.

HAUNTING THE INTERNET SINCE 1999

The Internet is an amazing thing. It's like this place that's not a place where people who are scattered all over the world can nevertheless gather together in order to converse, share ideas, and even swap pictures, music, and video. With the advances made on the Internet since its inception, it's easy to create virtual clubs and other spaces for people to gather. There's a webpage for just about everything (including some things we wish we'd never seen), so why not a virtual village devotedly entirely to ghosts?

Ghost Village had its debut in 1999, appropriately enough, on Halloween. Founded by author Jeff Belanger (who is, incidentally, no relation to this author, despite the matching patronyms) who often signs his missives as the "Mayor of Ghost Village," the site was originally intended to provide a place for Jeff's articles on ghosts and hauntings. Obviously, the site grew, becoming a massive resource where all members can swap information about the nature of spirits and share their haunting experiences.

According to both Google.com and Amazon.com, Ghost Village is the web's most popular paranormal destination, receiving over 150,000 hits daily. The site is home to more articles and features than one can easily absorb in one sitting: member submissions on everything aspect of ghostly phenomenon imaginable, Internet radio shows like *The Ghost Chronicles,* and certification courses in parapsychology courtesy of Dr. Loyd Auerbach, "Professor Paranormal" (who is one of the few folks active in the paranormal community to have a degree in parapsychology from an accredited university).

The site really is a gem, and it is especially valuable for ghost hunting folk who may not have like-minded people in their actual geographic area. No matter how remote or isolated one might be, as long as they have an Internet connection, any aspiring paranormal investigator can hop onto Ghost Village and find a safe, fun, and knowledgeable community.

ART FROM BEYOND THE GRAVE

Spirit communication has played a bigger role in the lives of influential figures than standard history books are willing to let on. Consider the artist William Blake. Most people are familiar with his work as a poet, as he penned such oft-quoted stanzas as:

> "Tyger Tyger, burning bright,
> In the forests of the night;
> What immortal hand or eye,
> Could frame thy fearful symmetry?"

However, Blake's poetry and art went hand-in-hand. He treated all of his books of poetry like illuminated manuscripts, crafting the letters alongside the illustrations to create vibrant and interconnected works of art.

Almost all of his books of poetry were printed using a technique known as relief etching, sometimes also known as illuminated printing. This involved writing the text of the poems on copper plates with pens and brushes, using an acid-resistant medium. The plates were then washed in acid, dissolving the untreated copper and leaving behind a raised design. Each page printed from this method had to be hand-colored using water colors, which Blake did before stitching the whole together to make up a functional volume.

All in all, relief etching is a complicated and laborious method that requires a great deal of knowledge and skill. Blake began experimenting with the method in 1788, and he claimed to have had a good teacher -- his brother Robert.

It's not uncommon for an older brother to pass knowledge of a craft down to a younger sibling, but Robert had died in 1787. Blake insisted that Robert appeared in visions to instruct him from beyond the grave.

Post-mortem communication seems to have run in the family. Following Blake's own death in 1827, his wife Catherine maintained contact with him for the rest of her life. Catherine Blake claimed that the dead poet sat with her for two to three hours every day, and she looked forward to these meetings eagerly. She also refused to engage in any business transaction concerning his work until she had a chance to consult her dead husband first. His death was no obstacle for the couple when it came to handling their daily affairs.

Christopher Columbus Discovers a UFO

While on board his flagship, the Santa Maria, shortly before his (re)discovery of the New World, explorer Christopher Columbus bore witness to something strange in the skies – and dutifully recorded it in his ship's log.

It was around ten PM on October eleventh, 1492 – scant hours before Columbus and his ships sighted land – that the strange object was seen glinting in the sky. Columbus was first to notice the object, which did not appear like any star. In his own words, the object was "a light glimmering at a great distance." He called Pedro Gutierrez from below decks to verify his sighting.

The object vanished and reappeared several times throughout the night. As the crew of the Santa Maria watched, the mystery light seemed to dance up and down "in sudden and passing gleams." Columbus took the appearance of the mysterious light as a portent that they would soon discover land, although why he connected the light with land is not recorded in his log.

Whatever the nature of the glimmering object in the sky might have been that night, Columbus's assumption about land proved correct. A mere four hours after its appearance, he and his shipmates had their first glimpse of the West Indies.

The sailors on the Santa Maria and her sister ships had braved uncharted waters in search of new territory. When they first set out, that territory had been little more than a legend. Was the mystery light that heralded their first sight of that new land some otherworldly beacon? Was it a visitor from an even stranger uncharted realm sailing the heavens on its own voyage of exploration? Or perhaps it was a light of warning appearing, not to Columbus and his crew, but to the people of the islands whose way of life was about to be changed forever.

THE LANTERN MAN

A tired and weary peasant is making his way home on foot late one night through the Welsh countryside. It's dark, and the path is rocky and uncertain, but soon he sees a bright light in the distance. Assuming the light to be a lantern, the traveler follows it for some distance, trying to catch up to the person who must be carrying this beacon of warmth and safety. After several miles, however, the traveler finds himself standing at the very edge of a steep precipice. The light hangs in the air before him, but had he continued to follow it, he would surely have plunged to his death.

This unsettling tale, recounted in Wirt Sikes' book *British Goblins*, is a classic encounter with a Welsh *pwca*, better known to many people as the Will o' the Wisp. This lambent faery light, which appears in swamps and wild places and is believed to lead travelers astray, is a phenomenon recorded over many centuries in and many lands. Here in the West, we are most familiar with the stories of Will o' the Wisp that come to us from the British Isles, where the lights are most often ascribed to the mischievous – and occasionally malevolent – activities of the faery folk. Although the most common activity of the Will o' the Wisp is to lead travelers on a merry detour through wild and waste places, according to some of the folk traditions surrounding these mysterious lights, they have also been known to lead people to hidden treasure.

Most tales of Will o' the Wisp imply a type of sentience behind the faery light, even though modern debunkers are generally inclined to explain them away as swamp gas or even a reflection of the moon on water.

Modern instances of faery lights, such as the Marfa Lights in Marfa, Texas, are often associated not with faeries but with extra-terrestrials and UFO activity.

The original faery lights go by many different names, depending on the region of the British Isles they come from. They're called "Spunkies" in lowland Scotland, "Hobbedy's Lantern" in Warwickshire, "Peg-a-Lantern" in Lancashire, and the "Lantern Man" in West Anglia. My favorite, however, is "Will the Smith," a type of Will o' the Wisp from Shropshire. The name is a reference to a traditional tale involving a wicked blacksmith doomed to wander the night with only one burning coal to light his way.

The Borley Rectory Haunting

Ghost-hunter Harry Price, born in 1881, was a controversial but highly influential figure in the early annals of paranormal investigation. An amateur conjurer who had an eye for fraud but a passion for serious paranormal research, Price was intense and charismatic and often was at odds with the more traditional members of groups like the Society for Psychical Research. Price distinguished himself with many investigations throughout his career. Every ghost-hunter has a favorite haunt, however, and for Price this was indisputably the Borley Rectory.

The Borley haunting both fascinated and frightened Price, and he returned to it again and again, both literally and in his writings. The Borley Rectory had a checkered past, as do so many deeply haunted sites. According to local legend, both a convent and monastery stood near the site of the rectory. In the 13th century, a monk and nun fell in love and attempted to escape to pursue their illicit affair, allegedly riding off in a coach and horses. As the legend goes, the pair were captured shortly after their escape. The monk was hung and the nun was walled up in the convent to die a horrible, lingering death.

The Borley Rectory itself was built in 1863 upon the site of the Benedictine monastery. The rectory first housed a Reverend Bull and his family. In 1892, Bull died in the rectory, passing away in a room known as the Blue Room, which later came to be known as the most haunted room in the building. The young Harry Bull took over for his father and held the building until 1927 when he, also, died in the Blue Room. The Bulls experienced hauntings in their day, including footsteps, a ghostly nun who walked the grounds, and doorbells ringing of their own accord. The Bulls seemed to take the hauntings in stride, and the young Harry Bull even joked that when he died, he would return to haunt the place in his own turn.

The next family to occupy the property in 1930 was far less sanguine about their spiritual co-inhabitants. Harry Price was called in, and he requested permission to stay on the property in order to conduct his investigations. He witnessed first-hand a range of poltergeist phenomenon. Price was involved in investigating the haunting through two more families, until the property was finally left vacant. During the years of 1937 and 1938, Price leased the property and conducted an intense investigation, which he later recounted in *The Most Haunted House in England*.

Some of the details of the Borley Rectory haunting may have even inspired Shirley Jackson's famous fictional work, *The Haunting of Hill House*. The intense, charismatic and sometimes misguided paranormal researcher of the tale (later played in a movie adaptation by no less than Cary Grant!) could easily be a portrait of Price himself, as he was often viewed as such in his day. And classic Borely rectory phenomenon, including scrawled messages that appeared mysteriously on the walls, found their way into Jackson's chilling portrayal of a deeply haunted house.

OUT OF THIN AIR

Many people have had small items around their house go missing, often in connection with hauntings, but what about instances where foreign objects mysteriously appear? Such foreign objects are called "apports," from the French word *apporter,* "to bring." The process by which these objects are apparently transported through the ether by ghostly forces is called "apportation."

During the height of the Spiritualist movement, apported objects were a mainstay of many séances. Numerous spirit mediums claimed the ability to make objects appear out of nowhere and they would produce everything from coins to live doves, much to the wonderment of their audiences. One medium, known as the gold leaf lady, demonstrated the strange ability of causing pieces of gold leaf to appear on her face when in trance. In modern days, the controversial guru Sai Baba continues to amaze and baffle crowds by materializing everything from religious statuary to full banquets of hot food.

A number of mediums from the nineteenth century were exposed as frauds, and their ability to produce items from thin air was proven to result from sleight of hand, but certain instances of apportation remain difficult to dispute.

In addition to its connection with spirit mediums who may or may not have been using prestidigitation to achieve their desired effects, apportation of objects is also occasionally connected with poltergeist cases. This paranormal ability may lie at the root of stone-throwing poltergeists such as the Drummer of Tedworth and New

Hampshire's so-called "Stone-Throwing Devil." In these cases, most individuals reporting such phenomenon tend to presume that the rocks and stones that are picked up by some mysterious force and thrown against a house originate from a nearby field. However, a Sumatran haunting witnessed and reported by Dutch explorer W.G. Grotten-dieck suggests that the stones have a stranger origin still. As his temporary home was bombarded by stones that began falling on the *inside*, he noted that no holes were made in the roof through which the stones could possibly have passed. Furthermore, he discovered to his amazement that he could not block the stones' entry with his hands. They continued to fall mysteriously into the building. Rather than being thrown from a point outside of the house, it seemed clear to Grotten-dieck that the stones were somehow coming into being near the roof and then falling to the ground.

MAPS OF ATLANTIS

Scientist Charles Hapgood risked his career and credibility in the 1960s to publish a book called *Maps of the Ancient Sea Kings*. This book is a study of ancient maps, some of which are in the hands of the Library of Congress. From these maps, Hapgood concluded that there was in fact an ancient civilization that was extensive and advanced enough to map out the entire globe with an accuracy that was equaled by our culture only in the 1950s with the invention of sonar. These maps are from the 14th and 15th centuries, and are copies and compilations of much older maps reputed to have been kept in the Library of Alexandria, and copied there from older maps still.

"Errors" in the coastlines and other details on these maps are consisted with them being copies of copies, and in many cases are actually accurate portrayals of coasts and river deltas that have since changed over many millennia due to weathering and change in sea levels. That these maps are truly ancient, and not simply products of the 14th or 15th centuries, is proven by the fact that at least one of the maps depicts the continent of Antarctica without its covering of ice.

We moderns had no idea that the coastlines of Antarctica on this map were accurate until very recently when we could use sonar to find the actual land there under the ice cap. In order for a sea-going civilization to map Antarctica without the ice, it would have had to have existed before the end of the last Ice Age. Furthermore, that civilization had to have been sufficiently advanced at that time to have the resources for accurate cartography as well as the need for an extensive map of the entire globe.

Just in case you think Charles Hapgood might be a crank scientist, it's worthy to note that his work was endorsed by no less than Albert Einstein, who wrote the introduction to his first book. Furthermore, Hapgood is still memorialized in science through the maxim of Hapgood's Rule: You only find what you're looking for.

Despite all of this, because his theories flew in the face of accepted historical timelines, even with the hard evidence of the maps, Hapgood's archaeo-cartography was swept under the rug by contemporary academics.

Hapgood claimed to have a follow-up book that would further challenge modern notions of our forgotten past and the catastrophic natural cycles of our planet. However, before the book could see publication, Hapgood was killed in a hit-and-run accident. His death was never solved.

COME ON BABY, LIGHT MY FIRE

In Stephen King's classic novel, *Firestarter*, the young Charlie McGee is gifted – or cursed – with the ability to light fires through the power of her mind. This rare psychic ability, known as pyrokinesis, has both fascinating and frightening potential. Connected obliquely with telekinesis, the power to move objects purely with a thought, pyrokinesis causes things to burn.

Some sites devoted to psychic development suggest that pyrokinesis arises from an ability to excite the very molecules of an object, thereby heating the object up until it begins to burn. Pyrokinetics are also allegedly able to control and extinguish fires with but a thought. The most common method of practicing pyrokinesis involves lighting a candle and seeking to mentally control the flame.

There may be a connection with pyrokinesis and certain Asian techniques, including a Tibetan Buddhist practice known as tumo. Through lengthy and focused meditation, a practitioner of tumo is able to raise his own body temperature to a point where he can sit high in the Himlayas and melt the surrounding snows. Some explorers, such as Alexandra David-Neel, who braved the icy heights of remote Tibet reported witnessing monks who were able to sit naked in the snow and dry wet towels applied to their bodies in minutes with just the use of this amazing internal heat.

Terror in the Night

You are lying in bed when suddenly you awaken to the sense of a presence in the room. Before you can cry out, this malevolent presence descends invisibly upon you, settling atop your chest and pinning you to the bed. You lay there, paralyzed and painfully awake as it presses harder and harder, stealing your breath. When the weight is finally lifted, you are left feeling violated and drained.

The incident described above is a classic hag attack. Believed by skeptics to merely be the result of sleep paralysis or a confusion of the hypnogogic state for wakefulness, hag attack is a phenomenon recorded by people from around the globe. Called *mara* in Old Norse, with a similar term in Anglo-Saxon, it is the very root of our modern word, "nightmare." While the Anglo-Saxon word meant only "crusher," and thus does not explicitly connect the *mara* attack with a supernatural entity, the Old Norse origins are very clear: the *mara* is a supernatural entity believed to sit atop peoples' chests while they sleep, thus suffocating them.

Researcher David J. Hufford feels there may be more to the hag attack than just bad dreams and sleep paralysis. In his seminal work on the topic, *The Terror that Comes in the Night*, Hufford suggests that "poor observation and incorrect reasoning cannot account for all reported supernatural experience." While he acknowledges that sleep paralysis and hypnogogic experiences comprise some of the classic hag attacks reported throughout history, a few cases defy these rational explanations. Notably, occultist Dion Fortune, writing in the 1930s, describes attacks by non-corporeal entities she termed "astral vampires." These beings, seeking to prolong their existence post-mortem, are driven to steal the life-force necessary for their survival from living human beings, most often attacking them at night, as they sleep. Fortune's description of such an attack lines up very clearly with classic reports of hag attack.

Is hag attack real? From Hufford's research alone, there is little doubt that individuals from all walks of life have experienced these frightening nightly visitations. Fortune's descriptions of astral vampires may seem the stuff of lurid fantasies, but enough cases remain unexplained that we can only guess at what entities or other phenomenon may be behind these nocturnal attacks.

HARBINGER OF DOOM

The sight of stone circles is a fixture throughout the British Isles, tied closely to the regions' Celtic roots. Associated with the Druids, but perhaps built by people older still, the great, lichened megaliths conjure images of a mystical past stretching back through the mists of time, older even than the Roman occupation of Londinium.

But that mystic, Pagan past may be closer than we think.

Rites involving stone circles – much smaller ones – are mentioned in the "Report on the Parish of Callander," written by the Reverend James Robertson in 1791 and later published in 1794. Robertson, who had been educated at the University of St. Andrews, was an expert both in agriculture and in Highland folklore. According to his report, rites were still practiced in scattered hamlets in his day, all survivals of the regions' Pagan past. One in particular stands out, as it seems to be the survival of a Celtic New Year's tradition.

Each year on Halloween, the neighbors assembled as the day began to wane. Earlier that day, ferns had been gathered, and these were used to make a fire as the sun went down. Ferns were used to light it and to keep it lit exclusively – no wood, and no other plant. Although the use of ferns is obviously significant, no explanation of this significance is recorded in Robertson's work.

As the Hallows-fire burned, each neighbor, according to his seniority, selected a stone and marked it as his own. These stones were then arranged in a ring around the ashes of the fire, carefully outlining the edge. Once the circle of stones was complete, the fire was abandoned and the embers left to burn out.

The next morning, everyone returned to the site. The stone circle was searched carefully. If anyone found his footprint in the ashes and his stone removed from its place, this was taken as a terrible portent. That man was doomed to die within the coming year.

DREAM A LITTLE DREAM

Dreams are fertile ground for psychic experiences. Even the eminent psychologist Sigmund Freud began to investigate the evidence for the paranormal content of dreams and, in 1911, his experiences inspired him to join the Society for Psychic Research.

One of the most commonly experienced psychic dream is known as the deathbed vision. Recorded by individuals around the globe, deathbed visions occur when a close friend of family member dies. The death may be sudden and completely unexpected, and yet someone close to that person will experience a dream in which the family member appears to say goodbye. In many of the recorded cases of deathbed visions, the individual who experiences the dream has no way of knowing that the person in question has passed away, even though the dream itself often coincides with the moment of death.

The ancient Greeks believed that the realm of dreams intersected with the realm of the dead, and thus the spirits of the departed could easily cross over from their realm to make contact with sleeping family members.

This notion that the realm of spirits coincides with the realm of dreams may also help to explain another type of psychic dream phenomenon: the announcing dream. In a typical announcing dream, a deceased family member appears to the dreamer and announces that he or she is planning to return. Women who experience announcing dreams frequently conceive shortly after experiencing the dream. Many such dreamers believe that a child this conceived is really the soul of the deceased, come to join the family once again.

HUNTING GHOSTS CAN BE A DRAIN

Planning a Halloween outing to hunt ghosts? Be sure to bring plenty of batteries! According to many paranormal investigators, ghosts and other phenomenon can be a real drain on equipment. One of the most common causes of equipment failure on ghost hunts is a sudden loss of battery charge. Spirits may possess the ability to influence electro-magnetic fields. Some researchers are so certain of this ability that they profess devices like the K2 EMF detector can enable spirits to communicate with the living.

One early twentieth century occultist, however, had other ideas. Dion Fortune, writing in her *Book of the Dead*, posits that ghosts need energy just as living beings need food. Following this line of reasoning, Fortune asserts that the traditional offerings left out for the dead, such as fresh flowers, are not mere tokens of respect. The flowers contain vital energy, and this can help nourish a spirit as it makes its transition to the Otherside. Spirits that linger beyond their time require this energy to fuel their manifestations, and sometimes they seek to take this energy from the living. (Fortune offers tips on how to protect from this in her classic work, *Psychic Self-Defense*).

Fortune is not alone in believing that spirits essentially "eat" energy. Famous paranormal researcher Harry Price suggests that poltergeists sometimes fuel their noisy manifestations by draining energy from the people around them. He cites an experience he had in a haunted house that left him inexplicably drained. From the many stories of ghost hunters who have had their equipment zapped, it seems people's vital energy is not the only thing spirits can suck up to power their nightly hauntings. Batteries are tasty, too.

Mind the Tommyknockers

Many have heard anecdotes about whistling when going past a graveyard. This practice – old enough that no one who recommends it rightly knows where it comes from – is believed to fend off any evil spirits that might seek to seize the traveler as they walk past the dead.

Whistling, along with several other methods of noise-making, was seen as an effective apotropaic – a method of warding off evil influences and ill-luck. The ringing of bells, the clapping of hands – and in some villages from simpler times, the banging of any household implements that could be used to raise noise – were thought to drive off spirits.

In some instances, whistling was considered unlucky, as with the French rhyme, *"Une poule qui chante le coq et une fille qui siffle, portent palheur dans la maison,"* recited in Normandy and its counterpart from Northamptonshire:

> A whistling woman and a crowing hen,
> Are neither fit for God nor men.

William Hendersen, writing in his 1866 publication, *Folklore of the Northern Counties of England and the Borders,* recounts a ship's captain who refused to allow one passenger entry on the grounds that the girl whistled. Her omen of ill-luck worked in her favor, however, as the vessel was lost and had the captain not turned her away, she would have been lost with it (and no doubt blamed for the misfortune).

But, in keeping with noise-making as a method for driving away spirits, it is interesting to learn that in Cornwall and Devonshire, whistling is forbidden in the mines not because it is considered unlucky, but instead because it is considered irreverent.

Irreverent to whom, exactly? Though not explicitly stated by the miners themselves, whistling in the mineshafts was most likely avoided out of deference to the tommyknockers and other various faeries believed to inhabit such places. To offend those spirits while working beneath the earth was a sure way of bringing trouble down upon one's head.

HINCKLEY'S LIBRARY GHOST

The sleepy little town of Hinckley, Ohio is a crossroads for the weird. The town's annual event is a festival called Buzzard Day. Held every year around the Ides of March, Buzzard Day fetes the return of turkey vultures to the town with a breakfast of pancakes and sausage. The turkey vulture is the mascot for the local elementary school, and the Hinckley buzzards have even been adapted as a logo for a local radio station.

In addition to its strange fascination with carrion birds, Hinckley also boasts a haunted public library. Located in the center of town, the old Stouffer house was converted into a public library in the early 1970s. Ghostly sightings have been documented from the time of the renovations onward, primarily focusing on a woman in blue.

In the 1990s, the ghost became known for her habit of throwing books off the shelves at night. Librarians observed that the ghost had a particular affinity for the works of vampire author, Anne Rice, including her book, *Memnoch the Devil*, which would be found thrown from the shelves on an almost nightly basis. Whether the ghost was expressing her preference or dislike for these works was never made clear.

OUT OF BODY, BACK IN FIVE

Robert Monroe is a modern writer who established the term "out of body experience" as most people understand it. Born in 1915, Monroe began experimenting with astral projection in the 1950s. According to Monroe, the out of body experience, or OBE, was preceded by what he termed the "vibrational state," a subjective sense of rather violent physical tremors. Once the vibrational state passed, Monroe found himself unstuck from his earthly body and able to traverse the world as if he were a phantom.

Monroe's vibrational state has been dismissed by skeptics as nothing more than hypnagogic hallucination. In instances of sleep paralysis, for example, it is not uncommon to experience sensations of tingling, buzzing, or being violently shoved down into the bed. Similar sensations are reported in hag attack, which skeptics again attribute only to the natural physiological phenomenon that causes sleep paralysis. Monroe, however, disagreed. He saw the vibrations as the sensations of the light body as it separated from its physical vessel. Monroe was certainly not alone in his belief that humans possess a form beyond that of their physical body. Drawing upon ideas culled from ancient traditions the world over, occultists throughout the 19th and 20th centuries wrote extensively about the properties of this astral or subtle body.

In his experiments, Robert Monroe reports several out of body visits to friends in an attempt to communicate a specific message and therefore verify his experience. However, early on Monroe realized that, in the projected state, he interacted with the physical world much like a ghost. Similarly, as with ghosts, most embodied beings remained insensible to his presence. People who are naturally psychic may notice something amiss, although, much like a latent psychic responding to the presence of a ghost, there is no guarantee that the sensitive individual will fully understand what is being sensed.

Animals, however, may have a leg up on humans. In an experiment run in the 1970s Dr. Robert Morris, an experienced astral traveler, Keith Harary, was asked to project into a target room that was filled with all manner of apparatus to record energetic fluctuations that might accompany his projection.

One piece of sensory "equipment" was far less technical than the rest. This was a kitten named Spirit. Lonely little Spirit meowed piteously from the cold metal cage that housed him in the apparatus room. The only times that Spirit quieted down was when Harary supposedly projected into the room. Although he could do nothing to inspire a reaction from any of the technical gadgets, Harary's projected self at least could stop a kitten from crying.

STRANGER THAN FICTION

Good authors write from life, drawing upon the places and people that they know, and yet some authors seem to draw more from an uncanny knowledge of future events than anything else. In 1898, novelist Morgan Robertson penned *Futility*, a tale about a ship called the *Titan*. In his book, this massive ocean-liner was described as "the safest vessel in the world." Nevertheless, on its maiden voyage across the Atlantic, Robertson's *Titan* ran afoul of an iceberg. The resulting disaster sank the ship and killed many on board.

Fourteen years later, the *Titanic*, a massive ocean liner built by the Whitestar Line, set forth on her maiden journey across the Atlantic. Following oddly in the footsteps of the similarly-named yet entirely fictional Titan, the *Titanic* also ran afoul of an iceberg, leading to one of the greatest nautical tragedies of the 20th century.

In 1972 author James Rush, writing under a pen name, committed a similar act of unintentional prophecy through his sensational novel, *Black Abductor*. In Rush's novel, a young woman is abducted from a college campus by an inter-racial band of modern revolutionaries who have modeled themselves after Latin American terrorists.

The fictional victim, whose first name is Patricia, is the daughter of prominent and wealthy conservative political figure, and her kidnapping is described in the book as the "first political kidnapping" in the United States. Sexual assault that eventually becomes consensual is a fundamental part of the fictional Patricia's experiences in *Black Abductor*.

Author Rush's only intention was to pen a rather lurid (and, let's be honest: cringingly racist) paperback, so imagine his surprise when he was contacted by the FBI and later interrogated about his supposed connection in a high-profile kidnapping committed by an organization known as the "Symbionese Liberation Army."

The kidnapping victim was the daughter of Randolph A. Hearst, a wealthy, conservative, and politically-connected newspaper tycoon. His daughter was taken from her college campus by an inter-racial group of political revolutionaries, and she ultimately ended up aiding her captors. Her name, like the girl in the book, was Patricia – best known to history as Patty Hearst.

A Mother's Last Goodbye

In extreme situations, mothers are capable of amazing feats -- especially where their children are concerned. We've all heard stories about the mother who, after a car wreck, lifted a car to save her trapped child. In a story that appeared in Richard Baxter's seventeenth-century work, *Certainty of the World of Spirits*, no adrenaline rush can explain the strange case of Mary Goffe.

The year was 1691, and Mary, a young mother, lay dying. Mary had lived with her husband John Goffe in Rochester, England with her two young daughters. When the situation became grave and John could no longer care for his wife, Mary was removed to her father's home in West Mulling, approximately nine miles away. There, as she lay dying on the night of June 3, Mary's only regret was that she would not be able to tell her children that she loved them one last time.

At her father's house, Mary was being watched by the Widow Turner, a family friend. Between the hours of one and two in the morning, Mrs. Turner observed that Mary had fallen into some manner of fit. She felt the end was near, as Mary lay motionless in bed, her eyes open and fixed and her jaw slack.

Back in Rochester, the widow Alexander, who watched after Mary's children, was roused from her slumber as a figure moved stealthily through the house. It was just a little before the clock struck two in the morning. Upon getting up from her own bed, Mrs. Alexander saw none other than Mary herself. In a fit of fear, the widow Alexander watched as Mary went to the eldest daughter first, then stood over the youngest, appearing to speak.

The specter of Mary seemed real in all respects, except that, as its lips moved, no audible sound issued forth. Once its message had been conveyed, the specter disappeared. The widow Alexander spent the next four hours walking out of doors, trying to convince herself that what she had witnessed had been a dream, to no avail: she knew she had been awake.

Later the next day, on the fourth of June, Mary passed away, but not before telling her mother that she could die happy. Mary herself asserted that she had visited her children the night before, saying goodbye to each while she slept.

MYSTERIES OF THE GREAT PYRAMID

There are numerous instances of archaeological finds that are thrown out or relegated to the dusty corners of museum basements because the facts they suggest are so extraordinary, modern scientists would rather pretend they do not exist than have to redefine their entire notion of world history and human development.

Among these is an Egyptian stela that talks about the restoration of the Great Pyramid as carried out by the Pharaoh Khufu, better known as Cheops. Cheops, as some may know, is attributed with the actual building of the Great Pyramid. This document speaks of the Great Pyramid in terms that make it clear it already existed by the time Cheops became king, and that it had been around Egypt so long by that point that its true origins had been forgotten. It was, however, viewed as a great and mysterious artifact, and so its restoration was a favorable offering made by Cheops to establish his reputation as a great and beneficent ruler.

Decried as a hoax, archaeologists prefer to believe that a stone removed from the Great Pyramid that has a red quarry mark on it is proof positive that the monument was built during the time of Cheops. What they often neglect to add about this is that the name of Cheops, as it appears on this block, is misspelled – and the misspelling is consistent with a misinterpretation of the hieroglyphs that was accepted as accurate during the time in which the stone was found. Further, the block was retrieved from the Great Pyramid by a fame-hungry treasure-hunter of ill-repute toward the end of a dig in which he had promised to find the secret treasures of the Great Pyramid and yet had still found not one painting, fresco, or hieroglyph in the entire thing.

Money was running out, and he had nothing of any archaeological interest to prove that his efforts were worth continued funding (famously, the Great Pyramid has no paintings and no hieroglyphic decorations of any kind inside). After sending all his helpers away, this fellow went to do some late-night work in the Great Pyramid within a shaft that he was sure would open into the real treasure trove. The stone with the quarry mark (in red ink that was still in use at that time, as it had been for thousands of years) was all he had to show for his long night's work of bashing through the ceiling. However, as the first "proof" of the true builder of the pyramid, the dubious find still made his career.

FAERIE CHANGELINGS

Come away, O human child!
To the waters and the wild
With a faery, hand in hand,
For the world's more full of weeping
than you can understand.
--W.B. Yeats

You probably know the poem, or at least the poet. Ireland's William Butler Yeats was writing in reference to a persistent folk belief that faeries steal human babies, often replacing them with a faerie-child instead. This faerie-child was known as a changeling. Changelings are often described as ugly, malformed, or just plain strange-looking children that reveal their uncanny nature through faults in appearance and/or behavior.

Beautiful children were at special risk of being stolen by the faeries and replaced with changelings, for the Fair Folk greatly desired to keep such beauty for themselves. As we're told by the Rev. Thompson in his collection of local lore, "Fair and lovely infants were the special object of their desire."

When a mortal child was whisked away, the faeries typically left something in its place. Sometimes this was merely a lump of wax or clay, shaped to look like an infant and imbued with the special glamour of the fae to appear to be a living child. However, this false infant would fuss and cry and quickly waste away, while the real child lived on in the faerie realm.

More often, the human child was replaced with a faerie. This changeling would eventually reveal its uncanny nature. Odd behavior was common, such as speaking long before an infant should be capable of uttering word. Several tales recount how a changeling was tricked into revealing itself when a suspicious parent referenced some ancient event – intentionally getting a detail wrong. The faerie changeling, unable to abide the mistake, would sit up and correct the statement, frequently adding that he'd witnessed the event himself – thus providing evidence of his great age.

Occasionally these changelings would survive in their adopted families to adulthood with no one the wiser, becoming adults often isolated from their communities due to their odd appearance and manners. More than a few of the collections of folklore reference fae-touched adults who are relegated to living in caves or abandoned houses far on the edge of the town because the "normal" villagers refused to accept them as a part of the community.

Because of the faeries' notorious habit of stealing babies, nurses would sometimes give a newborn a little salt to keep the Fair Folk away. In some places, a daub of whiskey on the infant's lips was thought to do the trick.

Jung at Heart

Born in Kesswil, Switzerland in 1875, psychiatrist Carl Gustav Jung was responsible for such far-reaching psychological concepts as the collective unconscious as well as the shadow, a psychological construct that is essentially the dark side of the psyche. In popular psychology, Jung's work is most commonly encountered through the sixteen personality types of the Myers-Briggs test. And yet, this father of modern psychology began his career with a paper written on occult phenomenon.

As a young man, the Swiss pastor's son conducted mediumistic experiments with his cousin Helene Preiswerk. His first published paper, *Zur Psychologie und Pathologie sogenannter occulter Phänomene* (On the Psychology and Pathology of So-Called Occult Phenomena) was based in part on his observations of Helene through their seances. The article, published in 1902, formed the basis for his doctoral thesis.

Although the title of Jung's paper seems to imply a certain amount of skepticism, the renowned psychiatrist remained fascinated by occult topics throughout his life, consulting the I Ching, studying alchemy, the *Tibetan Book of the Dead,* and reporting at least one incident of precognitive dreams where he famously foresaw the rise of Nazi Germany and its resulting devastation across the European continent. Many of Jung's paranormal insights are recorded in his *Red Book,* a massive, hand-written and illustrated personal journal that has only recently been released to the public.

ARE WE THERE, YETI?

On the night of November 28, Nepalese guide Tul Bahadur Rai was leading his band of American explorers back to their camp on the banks of the Manju River in the frosty region of Khumbu, in the Himalayas. The Americans, including monster-hunter Josh Gates, had come out to this frigid and remote locale in search of evidence for the existence of the abominable snowman. There are few other reasons that would convince American travelers to camp in this snowy region near Mount Qomolangma at a height of 9,350 feet.

At that height, the air grows thin and the nights give a new meaning to the notion of cold. Stories about the existence of the abominable snowman, a cousin to America's Bigfoot, have been around for at least a hundred years. Greek photographer, N. A. Tombazi, spied an ape-like creature near Mount Qomolangma in 1925, and famed explorer, Sir Edmund Hillary reported finding giant footprints near the top of the mountain on a climbing expedition in 1953. The creature, also known as a Yeti, is believed to be native to these snowy heights, a habitat that is often blamed for the lack of solid evidence for its existence.

As the American expedition had traveled all this way specifically searching for evidence of the Yeti, imagine Rai's surprise when he spied footprints in the snow near the tents. The prints, some measuring at least twelve inches in length, were of massive bare feet. Photos were taken immediately upon discovery, and casts were made of the impressions left near the camp. On November 30,

Josh Gates revealed a cast of one of the footprints as part of a press release concerning the discovery.

A Meeting by Midnight

One afternoon in the early 1900s, a college student named Hugh Callaway proposed a curious experiment. Calloway invited two of his college mates, Elkington and Slade, to join him later that night at a park they often frequented, Southhampton Commons. However, this late-night journey would not involve stealing out of the dorm rooms and sneaking across campus to the appointed spot. Instead, Callaway wanted his college mates to meet him at the park – in their dreams.

Callaway was better known to the world as Oliver Fox, the pen name that this science and engineering student often used when writing for esoteric journals such as the *Occult Review*. One of Callaway's favorite topics was astral projection, an out of body technique whereby an individual projects a second "body of light" to traverse the physical realm as well as vast and dream-like astral vistas.

Fox's experiment, which used the state of dreaming as a stepping stone into an astrally projected state, was, for the most part, a success. The next morning, Elkington told of dreaming about meeting on the Commons. He remembered conversing with Callaway, but the two of them waited around to no avail for their third companion, Slade, to show up. Calloway also recalled the night-time meeting with Elkington on the Commons, and he also noted the absence of Slade.

Slade, for his part, considered the experiment a failure as he recalled no dreams at all that night. Since both of his cohorts independently noted that he was a no-show, it seems that the failure lay with him.

SOMETHING BANGING IN BINGEN

Spooky little Carol Anne introduced most of America to the concept of the poltergeist in 1982, but stories about this so-called "noisy ghost" go back for centuries. One of the earliest recorded cases of a poltergeist haunting took place in Bingen on the Rhine in 858 CE. Recorded in a chronicle entitled *Annales Fuldenses*, this particular poltergeist was known for its stone-throwing habits as well as its penchant for setting fires. It also made the walls shake as if struck with hammers.

Flying stones, shaking buildings and even spontaneous fires have all been connected with poltergeist cases, but the banger in Bingen went a step further than most noisy spirits: it was said to also shout at people. The focal point of this haunting, a hapless farmer whose crops had been burned by the spirit just after they had been harvested, was denounced loudly by the spirit for a variety of embarrassing acts, including fornication and adultery.

The case got so bad that the Bishop of Mainz sent in a group of priests to exorcise the spirit. However, all attempts at exorcism failed and the Rhineland farmer continued to be plagued by the angry spirit.

X-Files on the Emerald Isle

Freedom of information laws are a wonderful thing. They let us – eventually – learn about all those weird projects our various governments would prefer to keep hushed up behind closed doors. Thanks to the freedom of information laws on the Emerald Isle, one of the most recently released nuggets of information is the fact that the defense forces of Ireland have kept a secret dossier on UFOs for thirty-seven years.

The dossier was declassified in May of 2007 and contains reports going back to 1947 – that same fateful year where, in the United States, a saucer is believed by many to have crashed in the desert near Roswell, New Mexico. According to Irish ministry officials, the dossier has been closed since 1984. Of course, conspiracy-theorists might well maintain that in another thirty or forty years, the freedom of information laws will bring about the disclosure of yet more recent projects devoted to tracking and analyzing this persistent and strange phenomenon.

Irish sightings include two extraordinary events in 2001. The first, a craft trailing smoke, was seen to crash into Benaughlin Mountain near Kinawley in February of 2001. No known aircraft went down in that area. On August 28 of that same year, a pilot flying over Cherryvalley in east Belfast reported to air traffic controllers at the Belfast International Airport that he saw a "large white light, circular" object "moving at high speed with no sound." The object reportedly was travelling southwest at around 3 AM. No explanation for the 2001 sightings has been forthcoming.

MUFON's Hollywood Hook-Up

As Elwood Blues in the Blues Brothers, he looked like your classic Man In Black -- black suit, black fedora, black shades. In the Coneheads, he played the displaced alien Beldar, making hilarious and sometimes pointed commentary on human foibles. Beldar and the Coneheads were comical products of the early Saturday Night Live days, but to Canadian-born actor Dan Aykroyd, real aliens are no laughing matter.

The fifty-something Aykroyd, also known for his role in the 1984 paranormal hit *Ghostbusters*, has been out about his belief in UFOs for years, publicly supporting organizations like MUFON and using his Hollywood resources to make certain that the truth gets out there. His latest effort, *Dan Aykroyd: Unplugged on UFOs* can be viewed online and claims to contain some of the most convincing UFO footage to date.

Not all interviewers or fans take Aykroyd's devotion to UFO research as seriously as he does. Aykroyd, who has won an Emmy and was nominated for a prestigious Academy Award, takes it all in stride, never faltering in his conviction that there is more to the stars than a Hollywood walk of fame.

THE DARK SECRETS OF SOLOMON

According to Biblical stories, King Solomon was the wisest of men. The successor of the much-loved King David (who slew the giant Goliath with a single well-placed stroke from his sling shot), King Solomon is credited with many wonders. It was Solomon who designed and built the Temple of Jerusalem, which ultimately housed the Ark of the Covenant.

Many myths have grown up around King Solomon's work with the Temple. The Knights Templar, first established in 1118 CE, took their name from Solomon's Temple. They made their base upon the Temple Mount and were rumored to be seeking lost treasures and artifacts hidden beneath the ruins of the temple. The Freemasons claim connections to the Templars but also to the masons who labored to complete King Solomon's Temple. Their mythic figure, Hiram Abif, may have historic roots in King Hiram of Tyre, a foreign ruler who provided money and materials to Solomon for the construction of his costly and elaborate temple.

If an extra-Biblical text is to be believed, King Hiram of Tyre wasn't the only person helping Solomon build his legendary temple. In the pseudepigraphal *Testament of Solomon* (sometimes called *The Wisdom of Solomon*), penned some time between the first and fourth centuries of the Common Era, King Solomon conscripts demons as slave labor for the temple project.

The document, written in Greek with a style reminiscent of the New Testament, describes how a young worker, favored of King Solomon, was beset by a demon. The demon, whose name was Ornias, preyed upon the young worker, slowly causing the boy to waste away. When King Solomon learned of this unnatural predation, he prayed day and night for the Lord God to deliver the demon unto his power. According to the *Testament of Solomon*, the Archangel Michael finally appeared and deliver to Solomon a ring bearing a seal, said to be a pentagram.

Through this finger-ring, the Lord God gave Solomon the power of the demons that dwelled in the earth and preyed upon mankind. The *Testament of Solomon*, supposedly written by Solomon himself, claims to record for posterity the names and offices of these demons, as well as the angels that have the power to command and bind them.

With such a heavenly gift, Solomon wasted no time. Ornias was the first to be bound. Solomon not only stopped Ornias from preying upon the young worker, but he then saw fit to punish the demon by commanding him to perform menial labor for the construction of the temple. With Ornias' help, Solomon then called up demon after demon, including Asmodeus, Beelzebub, and even a form of Lilith. He questioned each, learned the angel that held power over them, and then commanded them in the name of his God to bend their powers to lowly tasks such as cutting Theban marbles, mixing clay for bricks, and cutting and carrying wood. The demons weren't too thrilled with this slave labor, but they were powerless to resist as long as Solomon had the ring conferred by God.

Although it is doubtful that the Temple of Jerusalem was actually constructed with the aid of demons, the *Testament of Solomon* remained a compelling tale, and its treatment of demonic entities, in particular the methods of calling and binding them, laid the foundation for traditions of ceremonial magic that developed in the Middle Ages and may also have helped to inspire the Islamic belief in Jinn.

THE GREAT LADYBIRD INVASION OF 1869

Charles Fort is perhaps the most famous champion of the bizarre, combing newspaper articles and other reports to demonstrate just how commonplace the strange and the bizarre can be in our lives. His extensive documentation of phenomenon such as rains of fishes, mysterious disappearances, and the inexplicable appearance of exotic animals in places where they had no right to belong helped lend this unorthodox newsman's name to all things Fortean.

Perhaps one of the strangest cases reported in his book *Lo!* involves a sudden profusion of ladybirds that invaded England during the summer of 1869. As Fort notes, that summer had seen a notable decrease in insect life, possibly due to a drought. Then, quite suddenly, swarms of ladybirds descended upon England from across the English Channel.

The city of Ramsgate was hit first, and the influx of bugs was so profuse that they lay in great drifts throughout the streets. Soon the people of Ramsgate had developed a new job description: ladybird shoveler. After Ramsgate, ladybirds descended upon Dover, Kent, Surrey, Shoeburyness, as well as London. The bugs flew in by the millions, pelting against windows like living hail and enveloping buildings in a crawling, spotted mantle. The invasion was reported in newspapers like the *London Times* and *The London Standard* as well as magazines such as *Land & Water* and *Field*.

Although the swarms of ladybirds seemed to consistently come inland from across water, as if traveling from France or Belgium, there were no concurrent reports of swarms in either of these countries. This led Fort to conjecture that the bugs were somehow slipping into out reality over the English Channel while in mid-flight. Perhaps adding to this theory of an insectile alien invasion is the fact that the actual species of bug puzzled experts. They were clearly related to English ladybirds, and yet the swarming insects tended to be yellow, with a greater profusion of spots. They were also significantly larger than the native species of ladybird that were known in England at that time.

By the end of the summer, the swarms were gone as inexplicably as they had come, and it only remained for the newly designated ladybird shovelers to gather up the putrid carcasses and commit them to the fire.

To Orb or Not to Orb

Orb photos. They are trotted out on nearly every paranormal site as proof that ghosts exist. These mostly translucent spheres of light appear singly or in swarms, and according to some paranormal investigators, each orb is photographic evidence of the presence of a ghost.

Where ghost hunters are concerned, orbs are like a religion. There are those who fervently believe that every single orb in a photo is actually a ghost, smiling pretty for the camera. On the other side are the disbelievers, and they are just as staunch. The disbelievers argue that orbs are nothing but motes in the camera's eye, flecks of moisture or bits of dust. And yet, of all the thousands of orb photos that get posted on ghost hunting sites across the Internet, there remain those one or two compelling images: orbs that seem very three dimensional. Orbs that glow with a strangely colored light. Orbs that move in reference to the other figures in the image.

What are orbs, really? Do we all just become floating balls of light once we move to the Great Beyond? As interesting as that concept may be, it seems unlikely that, in photos literally speckled with orbs, each individual dot is the visible representation of a sentient spirit-being. On the other hand, at least in a rare few photos, the supposed orb appears to be something other than a fleck of dust.

There's probably no good solution for the debate, and perhaps that's what draws us to the topic, over and over again. Orbs represent that special brand of compelling almost-evidence that drives the continued search for proof. Because orb photos can be argued and dismissed, they keep paranormal investigators searching for that one perfect experience: the image of irrefutable proof captured on film that will make the world see – and believe.

GHOST-SPOTTING

Paul Rowland of the UK believes that cutting edge technology will help us to capture convincing photographic evidence of ghosts. The founder of *Paradox Electronics* was inspired by Sentinel detection systems which use highly sensitive sensor arrays in conjunction with both cameras and camcorders. The sensors detect movement, but they can also detect changes in electric and magnetic fields. A number of paranormal investigators believe that these energetic fields are affected by the presence of spirits.

Rowland's technology was put to the test during a ghost-hunt at Warrington in Cheshire, with intriguing results. An image that seems to show a ghostly presence, possibly with two glowing eyes, was captured using Paul's technology. Strengthening the case that this is indeed photographic evidence of a ghost, the image was taken immediately following an experience by a spirit medium. Although he is understandably excited about the image, Rowland himself cautions ghost hunters to remain objective when gathering evidence. Even so, the wicked alchemy of his ultra-hi-tech equipment may yet lead to the "ultimate ghost picture."

Phantoms and Feast Days

While it may seem a bit morbid to our modern sensibilities, an old tradition hangs around the night before the Feast of Saint Mark – April 25. In Yorkshire, Scarborough, Teesdale and related locales across the English countryside, those curious to see the shades of the people fated to die in the coming year would keep vigil at the entrance of the town church.

The vigil traditionally lasted for an hour before midnight and an hour afterward. The procession of spirits would not appear unless the vigil-keeper spent the full two hours, awake and watchful. Falling asleep during the vigil was believed to have dire consequences – far worse than merely losing the opportunity to see the solemn parade of future dead. It was said that any who fell asleep while keeping this vigil guaranteed themselves a place among the spirits' ranks and therefore would be dead within the year.

By some accounts, it was necessary to keep the vigil for three consecutive years before the parade of phantoms would present itself to the observer. In the West Riding of Yorkshire, a variation of this practice places the date of the vigil not on Saint Mark's Eve, but on the Eve of All Saints – a date far more in tune with our modern sensibilities. All Saints Day falls on November first. This feast day is sometimes also called All Hallows, and the evening before it is widely celebrated as Halloween.

If, like me, you're a geek of a certain age, you might have caught the short-lived Chris Carter television series *Millennium*. In that show, which built upon a wide variety of folk beliefs and superstitions, the main character and his daughter, both gifted with psychic sensitivities, arrive through happenstance at the doors of their local church just in time to see the procession of shades on the Eve of All Saints.

The All Hallows' version was the one recounted to me by my spinster Great-Aunt, who was the self-proclaimed keeper of all things Irish in her little branch of clan Mahoney, originally from County Cork.

GHOSTS OVER ROSWELL

Shouldn't that be UFOs? Maybe – if we were talking about Roswell, New Mexico. However, in Roswell, Georgia, ghosts are the paranormal phenomenon of choice and the members of the Roswell Ghost Tour will happily tell you all about the spectral residents of their town. Located just north of Atlanta, Roswell, GA, is a quaint little city with a lot of history. Overlooking the town from the highest vantage point is the serene and majestic Barrington Hall, considered to be one of the best examples of Greek revival architecture in the US. Another fine antebellum edifice is Bulloch Hall, a building that was once home to Mittie Bulloch, the mother of 26th President Teddy Roosevelt.

Roswell would be worth a visit for all the history waiting to be discovered along its quiet streets, but the town also seems to have a high penchant for paranormal phenomenon. Dianna Aveena and her husband Joe, the owners of the tour, are both long-time Roswell residents whose own ghostly experiences inspired their involvement in the tour.

Avid ghost-hunters themselves, the Aveenas pursue their spectral neighbors through a combination of technology and intuitive perceptions. They get a lot of encouragement from their living neighbors who regularly volunteer stories of their own ghostly encounters in the haunted town. Avoiding cheesy stunts or theatrics, the Roswell Ghost Tour relies on the ghosts themselves to add spice to their nightly excursions. Judging by the number of intuitive perceptions, EVPs, and weird photographs generated from the tour I recently attended, I would say that Roswell's ghostly inhabitants don't disappoint.

THE HASEROT ANGEL

Tucked away in the rolling, wooded hills of Cleveland, Ohio's 285-acre Lake View Cemetery is a somber angel of weathered bronze. Expertly sculpted by Herman N. Matzen in 1923, the nearly life-sized angel with outspread wings sits enthroned above the plot of Francis Henry Haserot and his dear wife, Sarah. Scarred by pollution and the passing of the years, the angel's face has undergone an eerie change and appears to be weeping black tears. This quirk alone would render the monument imposing at the very least, and yet local ghost-hunters insist that there is more to "Cleveland's Angel of Death" than simple artistry.

Psychic Sonya, who runs Cleveland's Haunted Tours, has mentioned the Haserot angel when discussing some of the more haunted places in Cleveland. Mike LaRiche, coordinator of Cleveland's Paranormal Roundtable, has visited the angel several times. In Mike's opinion, "there is definitely something paranormal about that statue. I could feel the hairs raising on my arms as I approached it, and when I touched it, my hand came away tingling. It was truly an eerie encounter!"

Another psychic who has experienced the spirit of the grim monument is the young Sarah Davis. While attending the College of Wooster, Davis led ghost tours in Wayne County, considered by many to be the most haunted county in Ohio. When the Haserot Angel was brought to her attention, Davis identified the statue as no ordinary haunting. Rather than perceiving a human spirit, Davis felt that an entity had come to inhabit the statue itself. This spirit-being, in her opinion, was definitely not human, although she did not feel that it was evil. "He's beautiful!" she said of the spirit in the statue, "But so sad."

The angel was commissioned by Francis Henry Haserot (1860-1953) to watch over the grave of his wife, Sarah, who had died in 1920. Sarah was very dear to Francis, and he remained a widower until his own death more than thirty years later. If Davis is correct and neither Francis nor his wife linger in spirit at the grave, what manner of being haunts the somber-faced statue?

The massive bronze angel remains impassive as it silently guards the Haserot family graves as well as its own dark secrets.

BIBLICAL BLOODSUCKERS

We all know that, thanks to Bram Stoker, the bloody Count Dracula swept into our popular imagination just a little over a century ago. But vampires were a subject of fiction and myth long before Dracula came onto the scene. Writers like Lord Byron, Joseph LeFanu, and even Samuel Taylor Coleridge had all turned their pens to the vampire tale at least once. Their writing, in turn, was inspired by vampire epidemics reported throughout Eastern Europe in the seventeenth and eighteenth centuries.

But how old are vampires really? Our modern image of the vampire owes a great deal to the folkloric vampires of Eastern Europe, but the concept of vampires may be far older than the risen corpses of the Transylvanian countryside. Even the Bible seems to have one or two vampire-like creatures lurking within its pages.

Proverbs 30:14-16 tells of a race of people "whose teeth are swords, whose fangs are knives." They prey upon the needy and the poor, and they are compared to the *aluka*, a type of horse-leech.

These Biblical bloodsuckers are most likely meant to be a metaphor for mean-spirited and predatory people, but the passage in Proverbs seems to present them quite seriously. Considering that the Nephilim mentioned briefly in Genesis were also said to drink blood, vampires may be a far older – and stranger – breed of beings than we give them credit for.

THE DEMONS OF DR. FAUST

Dr. Faustus summoned a demon, and it made great theater. On English stages at the same time actors performed Shakespeare at the Globe, Dr. Faustus called up the demon Mephistopheles and made a pact to trade his immortal soul. The playwright, Kit Marlowe, certainly embellished many aspects of the Faust myth, but much like his contemporary, William Shakespeare, he drew core elements of his diabolic tale from beliefs, legends, and real practices of the time.

Marlowe was writing in the early 1600s – a heated time in Europe for both demonology and witchcraft. Johann Weyer, (the student of Agrippa mentioned in a previous chapter), published his landmark work on the belief in demons and witchcraft, *De Praestigiis Daemonum*, in 1563 and it was still in circulation when Marlowe put pen to paper. The *Pseudomonarchia Daemonum* (or, "False Monarchy of Demons"), an appendix famously circulated from Weyer's larger work, makes clear references to the art of summoning spirits in addition to describing the extensive "false monarchy" of the demons themselves.

Unlike Mephistopheles in Doctor Faustus, the spirits of the *Pseudomonarchia Daemonum* are not presented as beings of fiction. Weyer wrote his entire opus as a response to the widespread belief in demons, witches, and black magic gripping Europe in his day. We know the period as the Witch Trials or the Witch Craze, a sociological phenomenon that lasted from the 14th through the 17th century.

At the time of Weyer's writing, individuals all over Europe were being rounded up, tortured, and executed on allegations of witchcraft. The vast majority of those condemned in these trials were accused of forming a pact – a literal deal with the Devil, typically for supernatural power. This deal often hinged upon the supposed witch's ability to summon infernal spirits in order to initiate the pact.

In hindsight, we know that the witch allegations were founded primarily in hysteria and prejudice. Women, outsiders, and religious minorities were frequent targets of the Witch Finders, and it was an added bonus for those zealous Christian soldiers if an accused witch's property could be lawfully seized and redistributed to the Witch Finders' friends.

The majority of confessions were obtained under the cruelest torture, and if a pre-Christian magical tradition persisted in Europe among the rural populace, the waters are so incredibly muddied by the baroque imaginings put forth in texts such as the *Malleus Maleficarum*, that sorting the true cunning men and women from their unfortunate counterparts has been rendered nigh impossible.

What we can say about the period of the Witch Trials is this: there were no Devil's Sabbats, no profane kisses planted on the hindquarters of black goats, and no demonic pacts the likes of which Inquisitors dreamed about. But the belief that spirits could be summoned – and exorcised, abjured, controlled, and compelled – persisted, and this was a far older tradition than the beliefs cooked up for the Witch Trials themselves.

OUIJA BOARD: ON THE BOOKS

Ever since the 1973 blockbuster *The Exorcist*, Ouija Boards have been viewed with near-universal suspicion. Depicted at best as risky portals to the spirit-realm or, at worst, overt tools of the Devil, this patented "game" of spirit communication has been centered in many tales of harrowing hauntings. But Ouija Boards did not always have such a negative reputation. Although the lettered boards certainly had their detractors, throughout the nineteenth and early twentieth centuries they were viewed by many as safe and valuable tools for spirit communication.

Named in 1890 at a rooming house in Baltimore by Helen Peters, the Ouija Board was awarded a US patent the following year under the auspices of her brother. Similar lettered boards had existed prior to this point, possibly as far back as the 1840s (Victor Hugo, who lived from 1802 - 1885, made extensive use of a lettered board to communicate with spirits, including everyone from Dante to Moses). Until the Peters family came along, however, no one had thought to seek a patent for the game. American entrepreneur William Fudd soon took over the Peters family business, and it was his savvy marketing of Ouija Boards in national mail-order catalogues that really made these turn-of-the-century items take off.

As Spiritualism was all the rage in the English-speaking world at the time, Ouija Boards quickly became must-have items for every medium's parlor and local psychical society. The boards were used to communicate with dead loved ones, but, more than that, they were often used to communicate with deceased celebrities. In the 1910s and 1920s, channeled books proliferated, each supposedly written through the use of a Ouija Board. Many of these were credited as the post-mortem creations of famous authors, including Mark Twain.

Emily Grant Hutchins, a woman from Twain's home town of Hannibal, Missouri, believed herself to be the chosen conduit for his post-mortem works. In the introduction to her 1917 novel, *Jap Herron,* she recounts her first encounter with Twain through the medium of a Ouija Board. Out of idle curiosity, she had attended the meeting of a local psychical society, only to have Twain come through on the board and begin asking for her. When she and the other sitters expressed skepticism about the spirit's request to have her start writing new works for him, he directed the group to check their records from 1911. Six years prior to any contact with Hutchins, Twain had previously come through on the group's Ouija Board declaring his desire to continue his writing career, but only if the right living person came along to transcribe his words. After this, Hutchins was convinced she was that right person, and she worked to transmit what she believed were the creative works of Mark Twain from beyond the grave.

She was not the only one who held such a belief. Sarah Taylor Shatford, writing in 1919, published *Shakespeare's Revelations by Shakespeare's Spirit*, another book purportedly dictated to a living writer through a Ouija Board. In the same year, Katherine Mardon Davis published *Light from Beyond*, a fictionalized spiritualist treatise that had also come through in a series of Ouija Board sessions over the course of three weeks.

Others claimed to communicate and faithfully transcribe works of writers, poets, and philosophers, including Shelley, Wordsworth, Voltaire, and Poe. Even Victor Hugo who had himself nearly a century before communicated with the spirits of the dead, was sought out to continue his work from beyond the grave.

Would the Real Vampire Please Stand Up?

Is vampirism a condition that exists outside of folklore and film? Are there real living people who psychically feed on human life force – or even on blood? What is the source of these supernatural hungers? The Atlanta Vampire Alliance has the answers.

Formed in 2005, the AVA is a research group devoted to the modern condition of vampirism – but Dracula would never recognize these vampires as kin. The vampires of the AVA are living human beings, often psychic, who have a need for the life force of others, and they have come together as a group to study and better understand that need.

This is no fly-by-night venture. The AVA's Vampire and Energy Work Research Survey, circulated to thousands of self-identified vampires and energy workers around the world, has hundreds of questions, focusing on everything from an individual's religious beliefs to the minute details of their medical history. The AVA's goal is to gather hard statistics about real vampires – statistics which they hope will ultimately be taken seriously in an academic context.

Part of this goal has already been achieved. Featured in the recent release, *Vampires in Their Own Words*, the AVA has also worked with several individuals attached to colleges as part of academic research. Most recently, they have started working with author Rosemary Ellen Guiley to help add their knowledge to the 2008 re-release of her landmark work, *Vampires Among Us*. The ongoing research of the AVA may very well change the way vampirism is defined.

THE GRAND-DADDY OF GOTH

More than two hundred years ago, on January 22, 1788, George Gordon, the man history knows as Lord Byron, was born. Of all historical figures, Lord Byron has had the greatest influence upon the Gothic and Vampire subcultures, essentially establishing the vampire as a Romantic ideal. His fascination with the occult inspired him to explore the folklore of Eastern Europe, and he almost single-handedly imported the vampire into Western literature.

Although Byron was not the first English writer to deal with the complex figure of the vampire (Samuel Taylor Coleridge beat him with his lesbian-themed vampire poem, *Christabel,* written in 1797-1800), Byron was most certainly the person who rendered the vampire immortal. This was not through his writings, however. It was Byron's infamous personality that helped shape the vampire as we know the figure today.

One of the first true pop celebrities (complete with a fairly typical celebrity stalker, in the person of Lady Caroline Lamb), Byron took the London social scene by storm. After the publication of his epic (and largely autobiographical) *Childe Harold's Pilgrimage*, Byron's name was a common household word in England. Charismatic and gifted, Byron's talents were part of his charm, but his flaws were the real root of is mystique.

A brilliant writer, Byron was also a deeply troubled soul with intense, tumultuous passions. Renowned for his almost feminine beauty (one biographer describes his face as having the pallor and luster of an alabaster vase lit from within), Byron's brooding reticence rendered him a mysterious and alluring figure – the very soul of the Byronic hero. He was "mad, bad, and dangerous to know," rumored to dabble with the black arts. Some even claimed that his clubbed foot was proof that Byron was the Devil himself.

Openly bisexual in an era where homosexual relations between men were still punishable by death, Byron was the perfect embodiment of the tragic outsider. His dress, mannerisms, personality, and signature androgyny have all become inextricably linked with the mythic being he first encountered on a tour through Greece and wrote about in the poem, "The Giaour." A dissolute lord infamous for corrupting his lovers, Byron is the vampire we have all come to know, far more than Dracula or any other written after him.

Paranormal Obsession

Media – in all its myriad forms – is reflective of its culture. And for well over a decade now, American media has demonstrated a distinct fascination with the paranormal: ghosts, vampires, werewolves, and everything in between. Superficially, this obsession may seem to focus on the macabre and outré – and admittedly, there is a voyeuristic quality to this paranormal obsession, a desire to tour the side show of reality, get a few thrills, then return to the comfort and relative safety of our familiar routines. But looking beyond the Barnum instinct of humanity, a more profound impulse emerges, drawing us toward the grotesqueries of shapeshifters and the undead: a deep and yearning question about the nature of life, death, and what we define as "reality."

As a culture, Americans in the twenty-first century demonstrate a growing interest in the metaphysical nature of our world. Issues of religion, the occult, Mayan prophecies, and the mystic potential of humanity all dominate our most current books, movies, and news. And, as odd as it might sound, nowhere is this interest more aptly expressed than in the phenomenon of reality television. One of the main concepts behind reality television – and its primary allure – is that it depicts real people in real pursuits. It has less of the polished shine of Hollywood and more of the dull grit of the check-out line of a 24-hour grocery store at 3 AM.

In many ways, reality television is the 21st century's answer to the Medieval Everyman (or woman) in that it reflects the audience back upon themselves. In that reflection, much is revealed. Reality TV lays bare all of our cultural fads and obsessions, and while some of those revelations are tawdry, not everything in reality TV can be reduced to drama on the Jersey shore. Ghost-hunting shows, starting with the iconic *Ghost Hunters* and expanding to include everything from *Paranormal State* to *Ghost Adventures* and *Most Haunted,* demonstrate an entirely different aspect of our cultural interests: our never-ending struggle with the question, *"Is there life after death?"*

The shows that are most popular are not necessarily the ones that give viewers the answer neatly wrapped with a bow. The real allure of the shows is the quest itself, and in this, they are an eloquent expression of our culture's current struggle to know itself, to understand its place in the world, and to contemplate where any of us will go when all of this may pass.

Faeries, Ghosts, and Aliens

Faerie lore is a complex and diverse topic, and its complexity is in no way diminished by the fact that different countries develop different terms and slightly different mythologies to explain similar beings. Here in the States, we're most widely exposed to the faerie-faith of Celtic countries, but practically every culture the world round has a belief in some manner of mischievous spirit tied to the wild places that occasionally interacts with humanity.

Although the "good neighbors" come in all shapes and sizes, most reports of encounters with the fae-folk describe them as diminutive, with huge, almond-shaped eyes. Their skin may have a green cast to it, or they appear exceedingly pale. Throughout the British Isles, certain places more than others are rumored to be haunted by the fae, and these are places where, if the unwary traveler treads, they may be whisked into the air and carried along by the faerie host. The nightly dances of the faerie-folk are sometimes marked in fields by great circles threshed into the grain where the faeries danced wildly in a ring.

These circles left among the crops are sometimes the only evidence that the faeries were present on a given night. The faerie abductees may never be seen again. In other instances, they are returned days or even years later, except to them their time among the faeries seemed only to be brief. Others who go missing have little recollection of what transpired when they were among the faeries, and their lost time is never recovered.

If these details of faerie encounters are beginning to sound familiar – from crop circles to abductions and missing time – they should. UFOlogist Jacques Vallée, in his landmark work, *Passport to Magonia*, draws comparisons between traditional folktales about faeries and the modern phenomenon of encounters with aliens. The reports often share things in common: missing time, abductions, midnight visitations. Vallée notes that many of the descriptions of aliens match classic descriptions of faeries – including several different faerie types. The familiar "little people," who are often depicted with oddly tinted skin, slightly oversized heads, and equally oversized almond-shaped eyes, share distinct traits in common with the aliens referred to as "greys."

But it doesn't stop there. In the faerie lore of the British Isles, the diminutive fae are only one variation of being among a large and diverse tribe. The Sidhe, sometimes equated with the Tuatha de Danaan (lit. "people of Danu"), are more frequently described as tall and graceful beings, fair-haired, with delicate features and porcelain skin. They possess an ethereal beauty that almost glows with unearthly splendor. These compare eerily to the blond-haired and blue-eyed aliens often reported as the "Nordic type." Even the reptilians and beast-like aliens occasionally reported have cognates among the faerie-folk who count kelpies and pookas, brownies and redcaps among their number.

Vallée suggests that reports of faeries and aliens represent people experiencing the same phenomenon but, due to differences in time period and culture, the acceptable metaphor through which they interpret that phenomenon varies. Greys and the "little people" share traits in common because the same cause exists behind both of these encounters. Country folk from the Middle Ages had faeries to put their experiences of lost time and abduction into context, while we in the Space Age are more likely to fall back upon beliefs in aliens and space travelers.

What is the actual truth behind the interpretive curtain? For that, Vallée suggests that we look past the temporal and cultural superficialities to examine what all of these reports have in common: beings perceived as outsiders. Are these outsiders faeries? Aliens? Interdimensional travelers? Or perhaps projections of our own unconscious minds intended to address a mystery deeper still.

For the moment, there are no solid answers, only more questions.

GHOSTS AND GRAVEYARDS

Graveyards may be devoted to the dead, but that does not mean that every person buried there lingers near their grave as a spirit. Many ghost-hunters will insist that ghosts are more likely to be found near the places and people that were dear to them in life. They argue that the spirits of the human dead are not so concerned about their mortal remains that they perpetually hover around their bodies.

This was not always the case. In the ancient Greek and Roman worlds, a great deal of importance was placed upon the proper burial of the dead. If someone died and their corpse did not receive proper burial, that person then became a restless spirit. The spirit would haunt the place where the forgotten bones resided, importuning travelers to find the body and give it a proper burial.

If a corpse were mutilated after death instead of being accorded proper respect, this would also result in a haunting. Several ancient peoples, including the Greeks, believed that the spirit of the deceased would exhibit the same injuries done to the body in the afterlife. This is why the Trojans are so horrified when Achilles drags the body of their hero Hector behind his chariot in Homer's *Illiad*, and why Agamemnon's death at the hands of his own wife, Clytemnestra, was such a pointed tragedy. Clytemnestra, in her rage, was said to have cut off Agamemnon's nose and ears in order to mutilate the Mycenaean king in the afterlife, thereby punishing him for eternity.

Top Five Haunted Cities

Planning a vacation? Next time you head out, try something a little less prosaic than touring the Grand Canyon or taking a cruise. How about visiting one of the most haunted cities in America instead? Although opinions vary from region to region, here is a short list of some of the most spooktacular places a ghost hunter can put on the vacation list:

New Orleans, Louisiana
Founded in 1718, this beautiful and historic city changed hands from the French to the Spanish and back again, producing a cultural mélange that distinguishes the city to this day. A city of magic, mystery, and voodoo, New Orleans is a perfect haunted destination. When you stop in, be sure to look up the grave of voodoo queen Marie Lauveau, and check out the new Haunted Mortuary, a paranormal observatory, lab, and museum.

Salem, Massachusetts
In 1692, witchcraft hysteria struck the small village of Salem, MA, ultimately sending twenty of its citizens to their deaths – nineteen by hanging and one, Giles Corey, pressed to death under rocks in an attempt to compel a confession. In this modern era, Salem has embraced its witchy history, to the point where even the local police officers sport a Salem-only patch featuring a classic witch astride a broom flying across a yellow moon. When in town, be sure to check out the Witchcraft Museum, but keep in mind that witches aren't the only thing you can

find in Salem. You can explore local tales of vampires and hauntings under the guidance of Spellbound Tours.

Savannah, Georgia
Founded in 1733, Savannah, Georgia claims to be the most haunted city in America, per capita. There is no doubt that this seaside city has both atmosphere and charm, with its moss-draped trees and architecture so reminiscent of New Orleans' famous French Quarter. Avid ghost hunters favor Savannah's historic Bonaventure Cemetery and the Pirate's House.

Chicago, Illinois
Home to the Shedd Aquarium and the famous Field Museum, the Windy City has much to offer an intrepid visitor. But this big-shouldered city has much more than mere cultural appeal. Chicago is also home to a number of famous hauntings, including the legendary Resurrection Mary. Also take some time to check out the haunted nightclub, Excalibur, as well as the eerie cemetery at Bachelor's Grove.

Hollywood, California
Grauman's Chinese Theatre. The Walk of Fame. The Hollywood Entertainment Museum. There are so many things to do in this city of the silver screen that a diligent traveler might not have room for all the ghosts. But Hollywood has its haunted side, and some of these hauntings are not to be missed. Search for the ghost of Marilyn Monroe at the Hollywood Roosevelt Hotel, and catch the ghost of actor Clifton Webb at the Abbey of the Psalms mausoleum in the Hollywood Forever Cemetery.

Dreams and Psychic Experience

Dreamwork was a full-time occupation in the ancient world. Artemidorus Daldianus, a Roman physician who lived around the second century of the Common Era, was one of the first individuals to take a systematic approach to recording the various meanings of dreams. He studied dreaming manuals from all over the ancient world, compiling what everyone had to say about this fascinating aspect of human experience. The resulting work, called *Oneirocritica*, or *The Interpretation of Dreams*, filled five volumes.

Artemidorus was writing about oneiromancy – the ancient practice of telling the future through dreams. Related to the belief that the gods could communicate with mortals in their sleep, oneiromancy relied upon the notion that many different levels of reality intersected in the realm of dreams, including shades of both the future and the past. Nowhere is this concept more eloquently stated than in the beliefs of the Australian aborigines. Their word *altjiranga mitjinai*, is usually translated as "the dreamtime," but it also means "ancestor time." The dreamtime describes a state beyond linear time where the age of the historic ancestors and the age of myths converge. Whenever anyone dreams, they enter into this other time where they might, at any moment, meet dead relatives as well as the gods of ancient myth.

Just as the dreamspace was seen to intersect between the world of mortals and that of the gods, it was also believed to connect with the realm of spirits. This is a time-honored tradition in many of the world's belief systems. Tibetan Buddhists see the gates of death and the gates of dream as doorways that open onto essentially the same space. In fact, they developed a technique called Dream Yoga that teaches an individual how to navigate the realm of spirits by first learning to work within the realm of dreams.

The notion that the spirits of the dead are able to traverse the dreamspace is not limited purely to ancient Greeks and mystics of Asia. One of the most common psychic experiences recorded among Americans is the death-announcing dream – a dream in which a loved one who has just passed away appears to say goodbye. All of this history shows us that, as a people, humanity does not find it strange that the dead can appear in the dreams. Based on the prevalence of death-foretelling dreams, it seems almost accepted that a person's spirit, once it departs from the body, is then free to traverse the non-physical realms – including the realm of dreams.

THE MYSTERIOUS DR. RUDD

Deep in the British Library, among the manuscripts of the Harley collection, there are several works attributed to an individual named "Dr. Rudd." Author Adam McLean, founder of Levity.com, appropriately calls these *The Treatises of Dr. Rudd* in his introduction to Rudd's own *Treatise on Angel Magic*.

Rudd was a curious fellow with an obvious interest in angels, demons, and ceremonial magick. Based on one of his writings, it is clear that he was also Hebrew scholar, sympathetic to the Jews at a time when such sympathies were hardly in fashion. He was, at the very least, an avid fan of Dr. John Dee, the court magician (and alleged spymaster!) of Queen Elizabeth I, and many of Dee's concepts are present among his work. In fact, there is such a huge influence of Dee's so-called Enochian Magic on portions of Rudd's work that Peter Smart, the individual responsible for copying the portions of Rudd's work that reside in the Harley collection, believed he was copying work that stemmed directly from Dee.

Aside from his manuscripts, little is known about Dr. Rudd. Scholar Frances Yates identifies Dr. Rudd with one Thomas Rudd, an individual responsible for publishing an edition of John Dee's *Mathematical Preface* in 1651. If she is correct, we seem to know his first name as well as the general time period during which he lived his life.

McLean, Yates, and many other modern scholars who have looked into the writings of this curious personage seem satisfied to believe that he lived and wrote during the middle and late 1600s. McLean points out that Rudd's *Treatise on Angel Magic* has portions that seem directly influenced by another famous book on magic, *The Discoverie of Witchcraft*, by Reginald Scot. Scot was writing in 1584, and at least one passage from his book seems to have been taken word-for-word by Rudd. This is a small section in Rudd's work entitled "The Hours Wherein the Principal Spirits May Be Bound, Raised or Restrained from Doing Hurt."

For some scholars, Rudd's apparent inclusion of this line by Scot is proof enough that Scot's work predated Rudd's. But the answer may not be that simple. A short comment left by Scot in the marginalia of his own work is taken by some to be proof that Scot copied Rudd, not the other way around. The note appears right next to the section believed to have been copied by Rudd from Scot. Here, Scot himself writes that he copied the passage from a book published in 1570 by "T.R." Could this be Thomas Rudd? The coincidence in the initials is compelling. And yet most scholars still believe that the man who authored, *Treatise on Angel Magic*, lived and died a hundred years after the date given by Scot.

Consider that the manuscripts in the British Library attributed to Rudd were copied by Peter Smart between 1699 and 1714. Thus, we know when copies were made of Rudd's work, but we do not really know when Rudd wrote the work himself. How old were the copies that Smart himself was working from? John Dee lived from 1527 to 1609. Is it possible that Dr. Rudd was not just a fan of Dee, but a contemporary? Then how do we explain the name on the Mathematical Preface dated to 1651?

Was the name "Thomas Rudd" or "Dr. Rudd" a pseudonym adopted by a series of magicians? Given how many books of magick are attributed to St. Cyprian or to Faust, stranger things have happened in the realm of ceremonial magick. One thing is for certain, the magickal writings attributed to Dr. Rudd, whoever this was, remain some of the most intriguing and enlightening of the time period.

HERE THERE BE DRAGONS

Every year, for one weekend at the end of August, aliens invade downtown Atlanta. They come in droves to see and be seen: Klingons and stormtroopers, browncoats and Centauri – creatures that have populated whole universes beloved by fans of fantasy, horror, and science fiction. The event is DragonCon, and, over the years, it has grown from a humble gaming convention to become a diverse festival of fandom that defies categorization.

So, what on earth are the Ghosthunters doing here? I blame the *X-Files*. Chris Carter's hit tv show made the paranormal a fan-phenomenon, and when DragonCon added the Mulder and Scully-inspired "X Track" to their programming, discussions about Star Trek's alien races appeared side by side with discussions about extraterrestrials, alien abductions, and UFOs.

It might seem strange to have paranormal enthusiasts at a convention so outwardly devoted to the scifi and fantasy genres, and yet there is a significant amount of cross-over between fans of speculative fiction and fans of speculative science. The SciFi channel hit upon this when they brought Jay and Grant's real-life adventures as paranormal investigators on the air. Now explorations into the world of the unexplained air in between old episodes of *Stargate*, and the SciFi channel has become one of the more popular choices on cable tv.

The crossover is clearly evident at DragonCon, where the X-track has been joined by panels that explore the reality of everything from ghosts to vampires. All are celebrated as expressions of pop-culture. The convention's guest list has similarly begun to attract more than just the usual roll-call of fiction authors and stars of old space operas. Patrick Burns of the Ghost Hounds Paranormal Network, author Rosemary Ellen Guiley, Dave Schrader of Darkness Radio, in addition to the Ghosthunters' Jay and Grant, are just some of the folks who gather to share their paranormal expertise.

Tens of thousands of people attend this convention each year, and many of the traditional scifi/fantasy fans come in costume -- so in addition to all the fascinating panel discussions, there's plenty of eye candy, too.

OMENS OF DEATH

In Celtic countries, the appearance of a fetch or spirit-double was widely believed to herald that individual's death – but it was hardly the only such fatal omen. In Ireland, seeing an apparition of the black coach was a sure sign of doom -- the black coach was the equivalent of hearse, used for conveying the coffin to the churchyard.

Henderson, writing in *Notes on the Folklore of the Northern Counties of England and the Borders* (published in 1866) compiles quite a list of other death portents from his countryfolk: phantom bells sounding in the night; circular lights appearing over the body of the sick person (in some traditions, called a "corpse-candle"); the touch of a cold and invisible hand, a disembodied voice calling a person's name; swords falling from their scabbards.

Additionally, there were many death omens associated with the appearance and behavior of birds. A flight of jackdaws or swallows going down the chimney was a herald of death in that house. Magpies flying in circles around a home also indicated that a death would soon occur. Ravens gathering near the house and croaking were also a sign – and if they gathered in the churchyard, they were awaiting a funeral that would soon occur in the town.

In Sussex, owls and crows are the favored feathered heralds of death. Three caws from a crow indicate that death is near at hand. The chilling cry of a screech owl at night also portends a death.

Not only black birds but white could appear as a portent of doom. Henderson tells of a clergyman from the town of Hull whose death was heralded by a white pigeon.

The bird flew round and round the house, alighting time and again upon the man's windowsill.

A farmer who finds an albino mole on his property is foredoomed to die. To hear a cock crowing in the dead of night is also a sign of impending doom. Cracking an egg to discover that it holds two yolks could be seen as a portent of death. Breaking a mirror was not only unlucky, but in Sussex, it was believed to bring death to the house.

Three butterflies seen together was also an omen of death, perhaps because, in some traditions, butterflies are connected with the spirits of the dead themselves (though this is most often an Asian, not a European, association). In Scotland, a piece of curled tallow in a candle was called a "death spale." Associated with the winding sheet in which a corpse was wrapped, this also was thought to foretell an impending death in the home in which the candle burned.

In recent times, Loraine Warren, a ghost-hunter with a particular fascination for demons, has popularized the notion that three knocks given by no human hand is a sign of the Devil, performed in mockery of the Catholic Trinity. However, in Henderson's collection of folklore, this sign – while ominous – is not expressly diabolical. It is simply another announcement of impending death.

Dreamwalking and Deathbed Visitations

Dreamwalking is where lucid dreaming and out of body experience intersect, a psychic technique of projection that allows a dreamer – spontaneously or through trained intention – to reach beyond their physical body to interact with others within the realm of dreams. While it may not always be named as such, instances of dreamwalking, where individuals make contact with others through the medium of dreams, have been recorded from ancient times onward.

In a related modern phenomenon, an individual dreams of a friend or loved one who comes to say goodbye in a dream. Later, the dreamer discovers that this person died right around the time of the dream. This classic experience is known as a deathbed visitation, and countless instances of such death-foretelling dreams occur throughout the modern literature of psychical research.

While the apparitions that manifest in deathbed visitations rarely reveal prophesies about any future event save their own death, they seem to have no problem crossing great distances in order to communicate with people important to them in life. This fact lends credence to the ancient belief that the dreamspace was somehow special and could be seen as a juncture of many different layers of reality. Accounts exist of mothers dreaming of their sons who lay dying, at that moment, on some distant battlefield, while young people away on travels often record dreams in which a parent issues a final farewell before succumbing to some unexpected illness hundreds of miles away.

A–Ghosting We Will Go!

Halloween is just around the corner, and ads for haunted hay rides and other spooky attractions are popping up all over. But with the current popularity of shows like *Paranormal State* and *Ghost Hunters,* who wants to go to a haunted schoolhouse stocked with costumed actors? Wouldn't it be more fun to investigate a real haunting?

These days, more and more people are taking up ghost-hunting, and the month of October – with all its spectral associations – is the perfect time to do it. But before you go out seeking spirits, here are a few tips to keep your experience as safe as possible:

1. **Take a flash-light.** There's nothing that says ghosts can't show up in broad daylight, but most ghost-hunters seek their quarry in dark and shadowy locales. For some, this is part of the thrill, while seasoned investigators know that it's easier to identify the source of mysterious sounds when fewer people are up and awake. Make sure you have a flash-light to help you navigate those dark corners!

2. **Bring a friend.** Ghost-hunting should operate on a buddy system, and you should never go into a haunted location alone. This isn't because the ghosts will get you if you're by yourself, but if you have a partner, you have someone to help you out if you get hurt. Also, you have a second witness for anything strange you might experience.

3. **Dress sensibly.** Ghosts can and do haunt five-star hotels, but most of the locations that are open to ghost-hunting are old buildings, like abandoned prisons or old county poorhouses. You are likely to get dirty, and you may encounter unpredictable footing. Dress appropriately. You may also want to think about pockets: a lot of ghost-hunters bring more gadgets than just a flashlight, and you need places to keep those cameras, audio recorders, EMF meters, and spare batteries.

4. **Get permission.** Although you may have a burning desire to investigate the ominous old cemetery down the street, most cemeteries are closed after sunset because of the real threat of vandalism. Don't get yourself arrested for trespassing. Check with the owners of any location (or, lacking owners, the local city authorities) before you enter a property.

5. **Have fun!** In the world of spirits, like attracts like, so if you go out expecting to find evil or violent haunts, you just might get what you're looking for. A moderate fear factor is part of the allure of ghost-hunting for some, but don't fixate on your fears. Putting out too much of that kind of energy can attract unpleasant experiences.

If, after your first taste of ghost-hunting, you discover you want to learn more, there are plenty of books to sate your appetite. Check out Loyd Auerbach's *A Paranormal Casebook* and my own *Ghost Hunter's Survival Guide*.

FETCHES, WRAITHS, AND DOUBLES

The belief in spirit-doubles – widely known today under the German word doppelgänger – can also be found throughout the British Isles under a variety of names. In Yorkshire, they were called "waffs." In Cumberland, they were known as "swarths." Throughout Ireland, they were called "fetches."

The fetch, like the doppelgänger, is not a typical haunt. These spirits are exact doubles of a living person. Their appearance was thought to portend that person's impending death. If a person should meet his own double, death could potentially be avoided by engaging it and driving it off.

Multiple stories survive of friends, family members, and even neighbors encountering the fetch of someone they knew. The spirit typically appears to all senses as real as the living person it emulates. However, on further reflection, the observer realizes that the person in question is miles away, or confined to a sick-bed. Often, upon this realization, the phantom disappears. The observer is left with a crawling feeling of the uncanny.

It is not uncommon for the observer to learn that the person connected with the apparition passed away precisely at the moment that the fetch appeared. In other cases, the individual connected with the fetch dies a few weeks or days later. In this, the fetch may seem to resemble the death-announcing dream, except experienced while awake. Many believers do not interpret the fetch as an attempt to communicate *in extremis* but rather a harbinger whose very appearance guarantees the doom of the resembled person.

The belief in these phantom doubles was so widespread that several famous persons give reports either of encountering a fetch themselves or -- in at least one case -- being terrified at the very possibility. One unlikely believer in this phenomenon was the English poet Percy Bysshe Shelley. An avowed atheist, Shelley nevertheless was near-paralyzed with a fear of encountering his phantom double. This fear is made more curious by the fact that his sometime friend and companion, the poet Lord Byron, was widely reputed to have a double of his own which appeared to friends and acquaintances in England while the poet himself was off traveling the Continent (others claimed this was not a double but the poet himself, mystically bi-locating through conscious – or unconscious – power).

That the Irish fetch is perceived as something separate from yet connected with the spirit of the dying person may derive from its essentially shamanic origins. Though the etymology of the term "fetch" is uncertain, it may simply be derived from the verb "to fetch." In this context, the fetch is a psychopomp, sent forth to "fetch" the soul of the dying person and convey it to the next world. Any encounters by family or friends with this spirit may then be accidental, as the spirit's real target is the person whom it resembles.

In Scandinavian lore, "fetch" is sometimes used as a cognate for the *fylgja*, a totemic alter-ego that certain people possess. They were believed to be able to project this animal spirit beyond their bodies. The practice of projecting an animal alter-ego to do work out in the world may have connections to later beliefs in werewolves, where, instead of merely projecting an animal form, a person undergoes a physical transformation.

Sailing the Ship of Dreams

In the Greek and Roman worlds, as well as in a multitude of other cultures throughout antiquity, it was believed that the realm of dreams connected the mortal world to the realm of spirits and the gods. It is because of this belief that the kings of ancient Sumeria would ascend to the tops of their ziggurats and there await a sacred dream that revealed the will of the gods.

Clay cylinders from around 2200 BCE are some of the earliest known records of this kind of divine dreaming. King Gudea, ruler of Lagash, wished to build a temple to his god, Nin-Girsu. As was the custom of the day, Gudea looked for Nin-Girsu's advice on the temple directly by seeking the god in dreams. Quite a number of dreams ensued, with Nin-Girsu as well as a host of other divine beings all manifesting to Gudea.

Oneiromancy was the ancient practice of telling the future through dreams. Related to the belief that the gods could communicate with mortals in their sleep, oneiromancy relied upon the notion that many different levels of reality intersected in the realm of dreams. Through dreaming, not only could mortals come into contact with spirits and gods, but they could also connect with the distant future and the distant past.

In Sumeria, contact with the gods through dreams was a privilege reserved for kings. By the time of the ancient Greeks, however, it was accepted that anyone could communicate with gods or daimons through dreams. The practice was called incubation, and people would travel from all over to famous shrines and temples in order to sleep in special dormitories, literally "sleeping houses."

The person seeking to communicate with the gods through a dream would make offerings and then lay down upon a sacred sheepskin to go to sleep.

Incubation was used to gain knowledge of future events as well as knowledge about cures and the nature of diseases. As an interesting side note, the Classical tale of Jason and the Golden Fleece is a remnant of incubation. Jason was sent to find the Golden Fleece because that particular sheepskin was considered especially potent for this method of divination.

Incubation was not limited only to temples or shrines. A number of tombs in the ancient world were considered ideal places to incubate. These included the tombs of the heroes Podalirius and Calchas in Apulia and the tomb of Trojan War veteran Achilles in Asia Minor. In these places, practitioners would make the necessary offerings, lay out the sacred sheepskin, and go to sleep, hoping the spirit of the dead hero would appear to them in dreams. Much like the visitations of gods and daimons, the Greeks believed that the dead could reveal hidden information and even help to cure worldly diseases. Dreams, for them, were far more than nightly fantasies. They were a potent method of communication, bridging this world with the next.

Harvard's Black Mass

A student group at Harvard will be performing a Black Mass on Monday [May 2014]. After the performance, there will be discussion about the spectacle and what it means in a country founded on – among other liberties – freedom of religion.

For those unaware of the ritual, a Black Mass is an intentional perversion of the traditional Catholic ritual of the Eucharist, taking the whole sacrament and turning it on its head. It is offensive to Christians and specifically to Catholics – and to be frank, it was designed to be that way.

During the European witch trials, there were plenty of allegations that the wild worshippers of Satan engaged in Black Masses. During the Middle Ages and early Renaissance these night-time orgies existed mostly in the lurid imaginations of Inquisitors and self-proclaimed Witch Finders. Their wild accusations provided fodder for later interpretations of antinomian activity, however. By the Age of Reason, some individuals did perform Black Masses, but these blasphemers were not serious Devil-worshippers. Instead, most were Atheists and Rationalists who sought to mock the religious fervor of their Christian peers in a time when they felt the devout should know better than to believe in demons.

In this respect, the Black Mass is an outgrowth of the Age of Reason – a loud, flamboyant and somewhat mean-spirited reaction to religious fundamentalism. Given the atmosphere in the United States today, it should not be surprising to see intellectuals going to such an extreme once more. In a country where we pride ourselves on our liberties – freedom of religion being a major one – we recently had a member of the Hindu clergy more or less shouted down by Christian extremists when he attempted to lead our Congress in prayer. Notably, he was invited to do this. That wasn't good enough for the folks whose notion of our country has skewed from the Land of the Free to One Nation Under God – a God who, apparently, must always be theirs.

The Black Mass then, and in a similar vein, the Satan statue that's going up in Oklahoma, courtesy of the Satanic Temple, is an equal and opposite reaction to this frothing extremism. It is a conscious spectacle of satire in the spirit of mock religions like the Church of Bob or the Internet religion surrounding the Flying Spaghetti Monster. It is also – though the utility of this remains to be seen – an intellectual exercise intended to make people think about what it means to allow anyone to worship however they please.

Civil liberties are at the heart of many of our hot button issues right now, with freedom of speech and freedom of religion in the thickest and nastiest parts of public discourse. The Black Mass at Harvard contains by its radical satire of an accepted Christian right a powerful question in subtext: if freedom of religion means any religion (including no religion), where do we draw the line between one group's right to worship as they please when that worship is directly offensive (or even harmful) to the beliefs of another group?

In a world that seems divided down the ranks of Christian, Muslim, and Jew (while any people who fit into the "none of the above" category get caught in the crossfire); in a world where the science show *Cosmos* is cut off the air in states that feel it should express, not science, but Creationist views; in a world where lawmakers speak with horror about the possibility that Sharia may creep into our system, only to turn around and pass legislation blatantly based upon Biblical Christian values, this is a damned good question.

Where do we draw the line?

Perhaps it's an older question than we realize. It may surprise most readers, but the Black Mass at Harvard hearkens back to the activities of at least one of the United States' founding fathers. In his dealings with Sir Francis Dashwood's infamous Hellfire Club, Benjamin Franklin himself may have participated in mock masses inspired by that Age of Reason disdain for organized religion.

ANGELS TO SOME...

The Seraphim are the highest order of angels – at least according to Biblical commentators like Pseudo-Dionysius the Areopagite and Saint Thomas Aquinas. The three-tiered angelic hierarchy promoted by both of these writers has become the most widely accepted view of how angels arrange themselves in Heaven. There are nine orders, or "choirs", and the Seraphim come out on top – a full seven ranks above the archangels like Michael and Gabriel. So, it may come as a surprise to learn that the term "seraph" may have originally been used to designate a type of demon, not an angel.

Biblical scholar Rev. W.O.E. Oesterley, who served as the examining chaplain to the Bishop of London during the early portion of the twentieth century, argues a very interesting etymology for the word in his 1921 publication, *Immortality and the Unseen World*. The term seraph comes from the Hebrew root *saraph*, meaning "to burn." Thus, Seraphim meant "the burning ones" – but not in a good way. Throughout the Old Testament, the term is associated with snakes. Oesterley first quotes Numbers 21: 6 to make his case:

> "And the Lord sent fiery serpents among the people, and they bit the people, and much people of Israel died."

The term used for "fiery serpents" here is literally "seraphim serpents."

Further along in the same passage, Moses is given a divinely inspired cure for the deadly snake bite. This cure involves making a "seraph" and putting it on a pole. Anyone bitten by the fiery serpents who looked upon the image of this seraph would live. This passage is taken by many to mean that the image is of an angel, but seraph is used again and again in conjunction with deadly snakes. From this, Oesterely believes it was not an angel but a serpent.

In Deuteronomy 8:15, there is a mention of "seraph serpents and scorpions" in the wilderness, and Isaiah 14:29 talks of a viper that shall come forth from the serpent's root "and his fruit shall be a fiery flying serpent" – which Oesterley again gives as literally reading "a flying seraph." From these readings, Oesterley argues that, at least to the early Israelites, seraphim were anything but angelic. They were instead theriomorphic demons that haunted the desert and plagued the children of Israel with fiery, burning bites. How the seraphim later made the transition from serpentine demon to heavenly angel is never adequately explained.

Faerie Tricksters

In France, the faeries are known as *lutins*. *Lutins* are described as little men, dark and hairy like dwarves, who live all day in caverns they have built underground. They come out at night and skulk about farms. Their greatest delight is in playing pranks on pretty young women. They hide their knitting needles, pull on their hats, and perform all manner of mischievous deeds. To this day, the verb *lutiner* survives in the French language and means "to play pranks like a *lutin*."

Much like the *lutin,* the faeries of the British Isles are renowned for their tricks. In Dartmoor, Pixies are reputed to take great delight in leading travelers astray, oftentimes getting them hopelessly lost in rather dangerous, isolated areas of terrain. Their favorite trick is to confuse the traveler so that he cannot tell which way is right or left and then alter the landmarks in the area through which he is passing when he is not looking. This is a process known as being Pixie-led.

Sometimes, the pixies themselves will take on the appearance of a particular piece of sod which would otherwise serve as a landmark in a long, flat stretch of land. The pixie-sod situates itself near to where the traveler is passing, then, when the hapless fellow is not looking, it will get up on its legs, run ahead a bit, and set itself down somewhere completely different.

In a similar fashion, will o' the wisps lead unwary travelers into dangerous areas of swamps and bogs. If the stories are to be believed, they tend to take a special delight in leading their victims into treacherous places that are likely to get them killed.

Even the darkest and most ill-reputed faeries, however, seem to be motivated more by mischief and a delight in trickery for its own sake than for any true malevolence. Death is simply a misfortunate by-product of some of their fun and games, almost as if they fail to comprehend that their mortal play-things are fragile in this way.

These dangerous pranks are not limited to pixies and will o' the wisps. According to faerie artist Brian Froud, the Irish faerie *Fir Darrig,* a kind of mean-spirited leprechaun, delights in playing practical jokes of a rather gruesome nature. Though many of the objects of his jokes wind up dead, the *Fir Darrig,* at least in his own eyes, is just having fun.

Dead Mountain

It is a mystery that has never been solved. In January of 1959, nine individuals went on a ski-hiking expedition into the northern Ural Mountains of what was then the Soviet Union. The hikers were young, healthy, and experienced. Many were students or graduates from the Ural Polytechnic Institute in Sverdlovsk (now called Yekaterinburg).

By the morning of February 2, they were aiming for a mountain known as Gora Otorten, about seven miles away from their current position. Sidetracked by a snowstorm, they pitched their tents on the eastern slope of Kholat Syakhl. Whatever happened on the night of February 2, 1959, it was bad. All nine people died far from the safety of their tent. By all appearances, the hikers had fled some threat, some of them succumbing almost a mile away from where they'd set camp.

Known as the Dyatlov Pass incident, Soviet police and military investigators never adequately explained what had happened. The abandoned tent had been sliced open -- not from without, but from within. All of their belongings were left behind. The hikers fled the tent in such a hurry that some were running barefoot in the snow. Others wore only socks or a single shoe. When the first two bodies were found, they were dressed only in their underwear.

Footsteps headed in the direction of a dense forest but disappeared. The two men initially discovered had died huddled around the remains of a small fire. Other bodies turned up shortly afterwards. These three corpses, including that of expedition leader Igor Dyatlov, lay in various positions between the fire and the tent, as if they had been struggling to return to their initial campsite.

At first, only these five bodies were recovered. All had died of hypothermia and showed no signs of violence. No one could figure out why they had fled their tent in the bitter cold wearing only socks and underwear, but it was all too easy to postulate something supernatural: The names of the two mountains are derived from the indigenous Mansi language, and both are ominous. Gora Otorten means "Don't Go There," and Kholat Sykhl where they camped is "Dead Mountain."

Two months after the initial investigation, the other four members of the Dyatlov party were discovered. The state of these corpses provided no further insight into the mysterious tragedy, although they certainly inspired more questions. These four, partially dressed like the others, lay in a forest ravine not far from where two of their companions had frozen to death around a hastily-made fire. But the remaining members had not died of hypothermia.

Incredibly, their bodies were crushed as if under a force of extreme pressure. There were internal injuries. In one case, a woman's tongue had been ripped out. No other external injuries were discovered. The police ruled out foul play, insisting there was no evidence to suggest other human beings had done this.

Later, tests of their bodies and clothing revealed traces of radiation. The measurements were small, but significant and incredibly puzzling. The official conclusion from the authorities stated that the nine people had died after encountering a "natural force they were unable to overcome." The case was closed, the results of the investigation were classified, and the public was denied any access to the site for the next three years.

What happened that night on Dead Mountain? Over the years, many theories have been proposed. The most popular -- and most straightforward -- revolve around an avalanche or animal attack. Conspiracy theorists blamed the KGB, suggesting that the skiers had stumbled upon some secret operation and subsequently had to be killed for what they had seen. Those who favor cryptids suggest that an angry yeti tore into the campsite, although no tracks save those belonging to the nine victims were ever found.

Lev Ivanov, one of the original investigators, blames fireballs. Although he did not come forward with this information until many years after the initial investigation, according to Ivanov, several eyewitnesses reported seeing balls of fire streak across the sky around the time of the incident. Writing in 1990, a full thirty-one years after the nine mysterious deaths, Ivanov suggests that the fireballs swept over the campsite, causing the group to flee in a panic. The fireballs then exploded or otherwise emitted some pulse of energy that killed the four wounded skiers, leaving traces of radiation behind.

There are as many problems with this theory as with any of the others, and Russian mountaineer Evgeny Buyanov has directly challenged it, insisting that there are no verifiable reports of fireballs, UFOs, or similar objects on the nights in question.

Will new information reveal what drove nine young people to their deaths on the lonely slopes of Death Mountain that fateful night? Or is the answer lost forever beneath the snows?

ABOUT THE AUTHOR

Michelle Belanger is an occult expert, presenter, singer, media personality, psychic, and author of over thirty books on paranormal and occult topics. Michelle has been featured on TV shows including A&E's *Paranormal State*, Destination America's *Paranormal Lockdown*, and the Travel Channel's *Portals to Hell*. Consulted for numerous documentaries and books, Michelle has also lectured on paranormal and occult topics at colleges and universities across North America since 1996. Michelle offers classes and weekend retreats on psychic development at Inspiration House in Oberlin Ohio, a 150-year-old home with the coziest haunting you could hope to find.

To learn more about Michelle's work, start by exploring MichelleBelanger.com where you'll find classes, books, music, and Inspiration House events. Follow Michelle on Twitter, Facebook, YouTube, and Instagram as sethanikeem or offer your support at patreon.com/haunted. If you are curious about Michelle's music, check out the album *Blood of Angels* produced with Nox Arcana.